ROBERT McALMON
Expatriate Publisher and Writer

ROBERT E. KNOLL

Robert McAlmon
Expatriate Publisher and Writer

university of nebraska press: lincoln: 1959

This work was first published in a series sponsored by the Senate Committee on University Studies (University of Nebraska Studies: New Series No. 18).

Publishers on the Plains

UNP

FOR V.

Foreword

When I first met McAlmon he was posing for a living before art classes at Cooper Union for $1.00 an hour. Sometimes it meant nearly a full eight-hour day. He had the straight, slim body, lean-bellied and not over-muscled, of a typical American college freshman. He didn't give a damn whether he was looked at clothed or naked by either sex so long as he got his fee. He got so used to the routine that when he entered a room he began to disrobe automatically, whoever might happen to be present. But this phase in his development didn't last long. He got tired of it. Its regularity left no room for composition; he wanted to write. He took a job on a barge of some sort stationed in New York harbor. That gave him time enough for his writing, but there were drawbacks of other sorts. There was no social life that he could enjoy such as he saw going on in Greenwich Village about him.

His narrow lips and icily cold blue eyes with their direct look left no question in the onlooker's mind that he meant what he said of any situation, and if any subterfuge was to be practiced he would have none of it. He spoke his mind under all circumstances and—with his keen, though undisciplined mind—you never knew what would be coming out. Some editors about New York didn't like that, and when they found he was sometimes not too sure of his facts they made Bob suffer for it. He was a fearless writer who never or seldom corrected proofs. That didn't go down so well with the men he had to face. He didn't correct even his spelling until much later.

All his earlier writing derived from men and women he had known in his school years. The stories were vivid portraits, really romances celebrating the goings and comings of the boys and girls with whom he sought to get away whenever the opportunity offered. Gathered under the title *A Hasty Bunch*, they show a young man interested in getting down what his companions were saying to each other in their daily conversation. It was their minds that he wanted to depict mainly, while dealing with the frustrations and inaccessibility of their beauty which affected him so intimately. The collection is a picture of the Middle West seldom equaled, but you have to pick and choose carefully among some pretty bad writing if you want to get anything out of it. *A Companion Volume* followed, and then the best of these first attempts at fame, *Post-Adolescence,* which is well worth rereading if for nothing else than an unwarped and unembittered estimate of the times.

McAlmon lent himself with unchecked vigor to the founding of a new magazine, *Contact,* whose name implied all the young man had most on his mind. He wanted contact with a world which theretofore had eluded him. Because his own poverty anchored him in one place, even though that place was a city, he felt the world was passing him by. Right at that time he was about to join the crew of a ship set to go around the world. The little magazine *Contact* had published no more than five issues when I received a letter from my old friend Hilda Doolittle ["H.D."], inviting me to meet her in New York. I asked Bob if he wanted to come along. There he met his future wife.

It was in the mid-twenties when the world was full of celebrities—among them Ford Madox Ford, James Joyce, and Ezra Pound—that McAlmon had his life's dream come true. He had always wanted to know the literary celebrities intimately, and to do something for them. Now that he had the opportunity with the old name of *Contact* as a masthead, he published a series of books, his own among them.

Paris was the center of the English-speaking literary world; everyone had to be as familiar with the Parisian byways as he was with his own back yard. The poems of Rimbaud and Apollinaire were thoroughly familiar to the Americans who frequented the Dome, more known to them than the works of any local celebrity. Picasso was just coming into his greatest fame with his Cubism. Everyone knew of the "Nude Descending the Staircase" after the famous Armory Show of 1913. The question of whether *Ulysses,* James Joyce's masterpiece, was going to be admitted to our mails was still being fought over in the courts. Everyone felt himself to be a rebel, the automobile was just about to transform the lives about us, Ford was the international hero. The enactment of Prohibition made us all drinkers. McAlmon led the pack. Everyone drank and drank heavily. This was the world into which McAlmon plunged; Paris was of course its center.

It is a curious note that in all the ensuing years McAlmon never took the trouble to perfect himself in the French language. He couldn't be bothered. He must have lost a lot that was said to him; maybe he expected to absorb it through his skin. He ignored London, though he was conscious that they were beginning to have their Eliot, but he brushed that aside—much to his credit—in favor of something of wider appeal. He was American to his very bones and wanted an American approach, bridging over any other connection between his own language and the inspiration of the French. He was a born cosmopolitan. Paris was more that than anything French.

The books that McAlmon began to write and edit now began to show his hand; and Contact Books were to be found wherever there were advanced books. This was the period of his most distinguished productions as both a writer and a publisher. *Distinguished Air* heads the list of his own writing. It is a brilliant piece of work, unfortunately all but unpublishable because of the nature of the material. With William Bird he established the Three Mountains Press in which, beautifully printed, the work of some of his most intimate friends was featured. (But I remember a battle he had with Hemingway, whom he distrusted. A train on which they were riding had killed and dismembered a cow. The two men at once got down, and Hemingway, notebook in hand, busily set himself to put down the appearance of the carcass. McAlmon was disgusted and turned away from the sight and gave his companion a disgusted look for his macabre interest in the affair. That was one of the incidents in the lifelong enmity between the men.) McAlmon published *The Making of Americans* by Gertrude Stein, an enormous volume of over a thousand pages. But the complete contempt which he had for all but the most distinguished of his audience made these books unavailable to the general reader, as they have remained to this day. If they could be collected it would make a series infinitely rewarding to the hardy.

After McAlmon realized that his best efforts to please an almost nonexistent audience had failed, he took more than ever to the drinking that finally led to his death. I'll never forget a party given for a girl, an advanced case of tuberculosis, who had been living about the quarter; it undoubtedly exemplified the kind of world in which McAlmon lived. He couldn't be bothered to look after himself. After a long illness, he died, impatient to the last, in Palm Springs, California, after establishing at least a speaking reacquaintance with his sisters, who had never abandoned him.

McAlmon was an abortive genius who believed good writing driven home would do much to make life worth living. He was fearless in his attack on false standards. In my opinion the book that contains his most mature and carefully planned writing to the best effect was *The Indefinite Huntress*. That is a book that could not have been written by anyone else, his masterpiece, showing the man he was with perceptions of life which show him to be a lost genius.

Robert Knoll's study is an excellent, well-written survey. Read it and learn what should be known about one of the least familiar and most important figures of "the lost generation."

WILLIAM CARLOS WILLIAMS

Preface

A year or so ago in connection with an anthology I was editing, I had occasion to read through many volumes of short stories. As is my habit, I discovered the obvious: the number of writers of the first rank is so severely limited that editors are forced by necessity to turn to Katherine Anne Porter, William Faulkner, Ernest Hemingway and Sherwood Anderson. I found that the drop from the first to the next rank is very long. After reading thousands of tales that are slick and contrived, I became convinced that integrity was more to be valued than rubies. Then a story by Robert McAlmon appeared. It seemed to embody a first response to an unhackneyed situation. Though I could see that this story, and his other fiction, was faulty technically, in it I thought I could detect an admirably independent mind.

When I turned to the standard histories, bibliographies and biographical handbooks, I could find no account of McAlmon, scarcely a mention. My curiosity was whetted. I began hunting for information, and I began collecting McAlmon's books. Both were hard to come by. This study is the result of my labors. Quite independent of the merit of my discoveries, the hunt has been great fun. I must thank McAlmon's friends and acquaintances who have responded to my inquiries: among others, Ezra Pound, William Carlos Williams and most of all William Bird. My monograph would have been less complete without the information they so generously supplied me. The McAlmon family has been very gracious, as has Professor Norman Holmes Pearson, who has in his possession McAlmon's private papers. One hopes that Professor Pearson will one day write a full-length biography of Robert McAlmon, placing him in his milieu. I want to thank numerous librarians for their help. First I must mention the staff at the University of Nebraska, and especially Bernard Kreissman, Assistant Director of Libraries for the Humanities, who has helped me in many ways. I must also thank the librarians at the Harvard College Library; the Newberry Library, Chicago; the Library of Congress; Lockwood Memorial Library, the University of Buffalo, the librarians of the Universities of Wisconsin, Iowa, Kansas and Minnesota. Librarians, I think, must be responsible for this country's community of scholarship. We are all in their debt.

Table of Contents

Introduction

Though Robert McAlmon has never received critical or popular acclaim, he deserves attention. An important expatriate in Paris in the Twenties, he was a writer, a publisher and a friend of the great and near-great who lived and worked there. He drank, talked, quarrelled with all of them; and we can understand them better for knowledge of him. McAlmon wrote a great deal, two short novels, four volumes of stories, four volumes of poems and a long autobiography. If these books do not earn him a place among the foremost novelists and poets of his time, they ought not be forgotten. His own publishing house, the Contact Publishing Company, brought out seven of his volumes; and it also brought out books by English and American exiles who became more famous than he. He published important work by Ernest Hemingway, Gertrude Stein, H. D., William Carlos Williams, Marsden Hartley, Robert M. Coates, Ezra Pound and others. Because of his activities as a publisher, as a writer and as a member of the Paris circle, he should be included in accounts of the literary activities of the Twenties.

McAlmon and the books he wrote and published are part of what Gertrude Stein called the "lost generation." He belonged, as Malcolm Cowley says, "to a period of confused transition from values already fixed to values that had to be created."[1] Other expatriates in Europe at that time did not remain "lost." Ernest Hemingway became a bestseller; F. Scott Fitzgerald has been turned into the official chronicler of his time; E. E. Cummings lectures at Harvard; Samuel Putnam translates Cervantes and Rabelais to great acclaim; Malcolm Cowley is a prominent critic and man of letters. The wanderings of many of the exiles ended. But McAlmon's search for certainty continued. He traveled over much of Europe and America, hunting for an escape from ennui, taking what pleasures came his way. All his life he lived

[1] *Exile's Return* (New York, 1934), p. 11.

with judgments suspended. Unable to embrace the religiosity of Eliot, the socialism of the early Dos Passos, the mysticism of the later Huxley, unsatisfied in Paris, Istambul, Mexico, he was constantly on the move; he was at home no place.

Like Thomas Wolfe, McAlmon found that he could not go home again. Putting down no roots, he continually harked back to his native prairies. Because he wrote of his memories of Dakota, Ford Madox Ford could say that he "represents—though geography is not our strongest point—that West-Middle-West-by-West of which we have been taught to and *do* expect so much."[2] Later he wrote of other countries, and new experiences, of Egypt and Turkey, of Berlin, and of Mexico. But always, whatever his subject matter, there remained something of the wide-eyed preacher's kid in his stories, even in those which dealt with the most abandoned lives of a disturbed postwar era. In almost all of them there is a freshness and a lack of contrivance. If his writing has a kind of slapdash that perfectionists can not countenance, it has its attractiveness, too. "Mr. McAlmon differs from all other serious poets of this age in being apparently quite without literary environment or background of any kind," Basil Bunting wrote in 1931. "It may be that this virginmindedness specially fits him to be the poet of America, the land without culture. Certainly what I know of his work has an air of authenticity while being foreign to the essentially European culture of Pound and Eliot. If McAlmon is not a great or accomplished poet or novelist he is at least a conscious pioneer of the American nationalism which has hitherto been prophesied but never effectively practiced."[3]

When all has been said, and much more will have to be said, there is a certain residue of permanent interest in McAlmon's fiction. If his village rascals are not Huck Finns (whose are?), their stories are told by a real man, a man of courage and astounding candor. He has an attitude, a point of view. "If the world's going to hell," he said in his memoirs, "I'm going with it and not in the back ranks either. So much can suspicion assail one's mind about the spiritual, the reverent, and the religious. My mind is not scientific and it is tainted with much bias, but such as it is it roots for giving materialism and science its day or chance."[4] His tone of fierce no-funny-business colors all his books.

In addition to whatever literary merit they might have, McAlmon's books have considerable historical value. First, they are of documen-

---

[2] "Communications," *the transatlantic review*, I, i (1924), p. 98.
[3] "Dictionary of Current English Authors," *Front*, I, iii (1931), p. 223.
[4] *Being Geniuses Together* (London, 1938), p. 132.

tary significance. From some of them one can obtain a truthful account of life in Middle Western villages before World War I. As such they add to what we can learn from Sinclair Lewis and the satirists. In other of his stories one can obtain an unvarnished picture of post-war Bohemian life in Greenwich Village, Paris and Berlin. John Peale Bishop has called Scott Fitzgerald's book *Tender Is the Night* the best picture of the life of the expatriate.[5] McAlmon's unsentimental account of life among the unrich expatriates is a valuable supplement to Fitzgerald's sympathetic slickness.

Further, these books have a use to the chronicler of taste. McAlmon was published in the best "little magazines" of his day—*This Quarter, transition, the transatlantic review, Pagany*—cheek by jowl with Hemingway, Joyce, Kay Boyle and others. Ezra Pound then and later praised him in public.[6] What was it, we may ask, that the editors of that time saw in this fiction? According to what critical canons did they give him such prominence? What standards did Pound himself use in praising his work? McAlmon's books are valuable as a kind of cultural barometer, for they can serve as an index of the taste of the period. Through a study of them one can get an idea of what this generation was trying to do.

McAlmon deserves our attention on three counts: first, because his books, besides being interesting in themselves, give us a picture of the taste of the time and of the societies in which he lived: the Middle West, Greenwich Village, expatria; second, because he was a friend of the most important literary figures of his time, and through him we can catch a glimpse of a world from which much important writing came; and third, because he was the most important private publisher of his day. Not attached to any firm but his own, not aspiring to found a syndicate and certainly not yearning for power, between 1923 and 1929, in collaboration with William Bird and by himself, he published a series of books by persons of considerable importance. During this time he worked harder than anyone else to distribute contemporary work that had not yet become acceptable to professional

---

[5] "*Tender Is the Night* is as complete a record as any yet written of the discordant doings of Americans abroad in that decade." "The Missing All" (1937), reprinted in *The Collected Essays of John Peale Bishop*, Edmund Wilson, ed., (New York, 1948), p. 69.

[6] For example, in "Date Line" (1934), reprinted in *Literary Essays of Ezra Pound*, T. S. Eliot, ed., (Norfolk, Conn., 1954), p. 82. He remembered to praise him again, twenty years later; cf. Dan Pinck, "A Visit with Ezra Pound," *The Reporter*, X (Febr. 2, 1954), p. 42.

publishers.[7] The activities of his press and a list of its publications have never been recorded.

After I have recorded the major facts of McAlmon's literary life, and before I consider each of his books, in sequence, I want to discuss his activities as a publisher and his relation to other publishers in this period. First, briefly, his biography: this gregarious expatriate was surely one of the fascinating figures of his generation.

[7] See Ezra Pound's letter to R. P. Blackmur, Rapallo, 26 March, 1925; *The Letters of Ezra Pound, 1907-1941*, D. D. Paige, ed., (New York, 1950), p. 198.

McAlmon's Life

The details of McAlmon's life are not easy to come by. Unlisted in the standard reference works, he receives passing reference in the memoirs of the Twenties, references that presuppose a knowledge which is, in point of fact, nowhere available. McAlmon wrote an autobiography, *Being Geniuses Together* (finished in 1934, published in 1938), but it is an account of only a part of his life. And in it McAlmon constantly disregards the historical sequence of events so that he may discuss an idea or a relationship extending over a period of time. It is a very readable book "in a down-right, hardboiled way," but it is difficult to use when after information.[1] A second source of information about McAlmon is even more treacherous. Almost all the "fiction" to which McAlmon put his name is thinly disguised autobiography. He constantly draws on his own experience for anecdote and plot. As a result, though one receives from the stories an understanding of their author's character and prejudices, one must hesitate to use them for factual information.

Robert Menzies McAlmon was born in Clifton, Kansas, March 9, 1896, the son of the Reverend John Alexander McAlmon and his wife, Bessie Urquhart McAlmon. They were of Scotch-Irish extraction. The family moved very early to a succession of small towns in eastern South Dakota. Among other places, they lived in Madison (population 5,000), Wentworth (population 300) and Volga (population 600). All were relatively close to the Minnesota border. Though the towns that figure in McAlmon's fiction are a compound of these three and others, he writes most often of Madison. Since McAlmon's father was

---

[1] It was published by Secker and Warburg (London, 1938), but it was never brought out in the United States. Desmond MacCarthy in a review of it, reprinted in *Memories* (New York, 1953), wrote (p. 117): "This is a piece of autobiography, entertaining in a downright, hard-boiled way, which makes the reader think he ought to know a good deal more about Mr. McAlmon than I do for one."

a Presbyterian minister, the family was impoverished. And it was very large: Robert was the youngest of ten children. Much has been written of the beautiful home life of large families—especially in those days of Gene Stratton-Porter and the Chautauqua—but McAlmon remembered his childhood as filled with discord. As the youngest of his family, he felt, without much justification, that he was frequently neglected and often abused. He grew up in this "wild and dreary plains state,"[2] stealing bread from the baker, working in the harvest fields, outwitting his elders. He played hooky constantly. He remembered that suspicion made even simple affections sordid there. Even as a child, he recalled, he was dissatisfied and longed to escape from this provincialism.

When McAlmon was in high school, the family moved to Minneapolis. His school record continued to be spotty, but he was graduated from East High in the class of 1912. One of his brothers, William U. McAlmon, became famous at the state university as a football player at this time; and later, when Robert was married, the newspapers confused the two of them. After graduating, the sixteen-year-old boy bummed around the upper Midwest, working in the harvest fields and on surveying gangs, settling down to nothing. At one time he was a reporter; at another, a copywriter in an advertising firm. But he found inside jobs confining, and outside jobs he found boring. Nothing satisfied him. He drifted. After four years, still undecided about what he wanted to do with his life, he matriculated at the University of Minnesota. But his family moved to Los Angeles, and in January, 1917, he transferred to the University of Southern California. Founded in 1879 and partially supported by the Methodist Church, at that time the University of Southern California had yet to attain great distinction. Though he was more attentive to his classes there than he had been at the University of Minnesota, he still refused to study. His father died in June, 1917. Though he stayed on at the University, participating in campus and fraternity life, dancing, reading papers in a literary society, he was supercilious. He thought his teachers pedants, artistic poseurs and frightened ex-ministers.

In March, 1918, McAlmon joined the infant air force. Though he was less interested in the cause to which the army was devoted than he was in getting overseas, he did not go far from home. Rather, he served at Rockwell Field in San Diego, where he helped edit a

---

[2] *Being Geniuses Together*, p. 157. The facts of McAlmon's birth and youth have come to me from correspondence with the McAlmon family. I have also consulted pertinent public records.

camp newspaper.[3] As soon as the war was over, he was released; and, returning to Los Angeles, he resumed his college career. During that winter he edited an aviation magazine in Los Angeles called *The Ace,* but it was not successful. More at loose ends than ever, increasingly he found the University of Southern California provincial. In a course dealing with the psychology of religion, he flaunted his independence by reading a paper that noted that fifty great writers of the preceding half century had been completely or partially agnostic; and, as a result, a scandalized fraternity brother attempted to have him expelled as a "heretic."[4] Though he had done respectable if effortless work before he went into the army, now he grew so impatient that his academic record became dangerously bad. By the fall of 1919, he was wholly rebellious. When he left the University in midwinter, he was on probation.

By this time McAlmon was attempting to write verse and fiction quite seriously. While in service he had published some verse in his camp newspaper; and in March, 1919, his first poems appeared in Harriet Monroe's *Poetry.* They dealt with his experience in flying. By this time, too, he had struck up a correspondence with Emanuel Carnevali, the young Italian-American poet who was an associate editor of *Poetry* for a few months (October to March, 1919-1920). In him McAlmon thought he recognized a freedom which he did not possess. Carnevali's full-blooded acceptance of the world contrasted with his own pinched and narrow, even effete, experience, he thought.[5] He became intractable, as he had in South Dakota and Minneapolis; and he left Los Angeles and went to Greenwich Village. Here his literary life really began.

Greenwich Village had been the center of avant-garde literary movements for the previous decade or so and had reached one of its climaxes in the publication of Kreymborg's anthologies of contemporary poetry in 1916 and 1917 entitled *Others: An Anthology of the New Verse.* Although many of the advanced writers were soon to move to Paris, in 1920 an important group still hung out in New York, and McAlmon became associated with them. One evening at a party given by Lola Ridge, an artist member of the literati, McAlmon met

---

[3] Dr. Williams says in his autobiography—*The Autobiography of William Carlos Williams* (New York, 1951)—that McAlmon served in a Canadian regiment (p. 172). There is no evidence of this. Cf. McAlmon's brief autobiographical note in *Americans Abroad*, Peter Neagoe, ed., (The Hague, 1932), p. 250. A picture of McAlmon appears in this volume.

[4] *Being Geniuses Together*, pp. 225-226.

[5] The "story" which McAlmon included in his *Contact Collection of Contemporary Writers* (Paris, 1925), "Extract from Spring Leaves Again to Consider," pp. 195-213, is thinly disguised biography dealing with this period in his life.

William Carlos Williams. Williams describes McAlmon as he saw him then: "Bob was a coldly intense young man, with hard blue eyes, who at that time found a living posing in the nude for mixed classes at Cooper Union. He had an ideal youth's figure—such a build as might have served for the original of Donatello's youthful Medici in armor in the niche of the Palazzo Vecchio. He got a dollar an hour, and was tough enough to take it for nine consecutive hours sometimes in various poses; he lived for a time on a scow in New York harbor to be able to make a go of it."[6] One of McAlmon's better stories, "New York Harbor," is based on his experiences on the scow Williams speaks of. Later he turned his experiences of Greenwich Village into a novel, *Post-Adolescence* (1923). McAlmon's first literary publishing came out of his friendship with Williams. It was the magazine *Contact* (1920-1923). Though it was edited jointly by him and Williams, for the most part it was paid for by McAlmon. In it the editors asserted their independence of authority.[7] McAlmon was behaving true to form.

By the time the first issue of *Contact* appeared, McAlmon had another interest which was to affect the course of his life. In its third issue (February, 1921) he and Williams had published an "Extract" by one W. Bryher. Miss Winifred Bryher had come to America from England the previous September with H. D., the Imagist poetess, intending to spend the winter in Santa Barbara, California. H. D. and McAlmon had a mutual friend in Williams, and one day Williams introduced McAlmon to her. Williams tells of their meeting:

"Well, how did you like her?" I asked Bob when we came away.

"Oh, she's all right, I guess," said Bob. "But that other one, Bryher, as she was introduced to us—she's something."[8]

H. D. and Bryher went to the West Coast and, very shortly, growing tired of eternal sunshine, began to plan to return to the East. McAlmon in the meantime had made arrangements to ship to China on a freighter, having found in New York little more to please him than he had found in the Middle West and in Los Angeles. He cancelled his plans when Bryher wrote him a card; and when she arrived in New York City, she proposed. They were quickly married and sailed to England on the Celtic late in February, 1921.

The surprising elements of the story, however, were not yet complete. It turned out that Winifred Bryher's full and legal name was

[6] *Autobiography*, pp. 175-176.
[7] A full account of this magazine is given below, in Section III, McAlmon's Publishing.
[8] *Autobiography*, p. 176. Dr. Williams gives an account of their courtship and marriage which is not entirely accurate, it is said.

Annie Winifred Ellerman, and that she was the only daughter of Sir John Ellerman, a shipping magnate, the heaviest taxpayer in England. McAlmon had inadvertently married an heiress. The tabloids gave the affair a big play. The New York *Times*'s account reflects the general attitude of the time toward Greenwich Village. Here is a part of the *Times* story:

'HEIRESS' WRITER WEDS VILLAGE POET

Greenwich Circles stirred by
The Romance of Robert
Menzies McAlmon

GIRL PROPOSED, IS REPORT

Bride Exploited as Daughter of Sir
John Ellerman, to whom Burke's
Peerage Credits Only a Son

Greenwich Village had a fresh topic for conversation yesterday: the marriage of one of its best known characters, Robert Menzies McAlmon, "editor and poet," of 351 West Fifteenth Street, and an English girl writer who indited a book of self-revelation under the nom de plume of Winifred Bryher.

But the Village talk veered sharply away from the official records of the Marriage License Bureau, which told briefly that McAlmon and Miss Winifred Ellerman—that is said to be her real name—on Feb. 14 obtained a license to wed.

Greenwich Village gossip was that the bride was wealthy in her own name and that she was related to Sir John Reeves Ellerman, the British ship owner, and some of this gossip even went so far as to say that the author of the revelations was the daughter of Sir John. According to Who's Who, 1920, and Burke's Peerage, 1921, however, Sir John was married only in 1903 and has only one child, a boy 11 years old. Face to face with romance, Greenwich Village was willing to admit that this took a little of the tang out of the romance, but it was still romance nevertheless, because—

The woman writer is reported to have proposed to the "poet and editor" because she became enthralled and entranced with a poem that appeared in one of the Greenwich Village publications. According to the villagers, she then met the poet at a party given by one of her friends. He whispered a line or two of the poetry and there was nothing to do but call a minister. . . .[9]

Winifred Bryher, born Annie Winifred Ellerman September 2, 1894, had published her autobiographical volume *Development* in 1920.[10] There is only one character in this book, Nancy (Bryher)—no other persons are considered, few are even mentioned. The author takes her chief character very seriously and assumes that her childhood trials and aspirations have some great significance; the account is singularly lacking in humor. The book had a foreword by Amy Lowell. Miss Ellerman, having become interested in the Imagist poets some years earlier, had written to Richard Aldington in 1918, while he was at the front, asking one or two questions. Aldington put her in touch with H. D., then his wife, and an enduring friendship resulted.[11] H. D. and Bryher traveled together to America subsequently; and after McAlmon and Bryher were married— H. D. and Aldington had by this time been divorced—they continued to travel together, sometimes with, sometimes without, McAlmon. The rather singular *ménage à trois* caused some comment at the time.

In 1921 Bryher and McAlmon went to London where, after living with the Ellermans in magnificence for a time, they took a flat. Character sketches of the Ellermans—Lady Ellerman who was deaf and temperamental, Sir John who was powerful and singleminded—appear in McAlmon's long poem, *Portrait of a Generation* (1925). While in England McAlmon met a number of prominent literary figures: T. S. Eliot, J. W. N. Sullivan, Harriet Weaver, Wyndham Lewis, Ronald Firbank. Though McAlmon reports that he got along with all of them well enough, they did not humble him. Eliot, he thought, was too full of the "snob-governess attitude"; he complained that "overcaution and gentility are so inherent in him as to stultify his 'intelligence.'" Wyndham Lewis McAlmon found to be waspish because he was shy and, as Lady Ellerman said, needed "somebody to look after him." Harriet Weaver confessed to him that "she feared she was a bit of a coward about 'facing reality,'" and yet she subsidized Joyce so that he could write the very incautious *Ulysses*.[12]

---

[9] Morning edition, March 12, 1921, p. 11. In a brief follow-up story, March 15, 1921, the *Times* reported that the baronet's secretary had failed to supply more information. "Inquiries have failed to confirm the story and standard reference books do not record any daughter of either the present or the late Sir John Ellerman." (p. 3).

[10] *Development*, a novel by W. Bryher, with a preface by Amy Lowell (New York, 1920).

[11] Richard Aldington, *Life for Life's Sake* (New York, 1941), p. 211.

[12] *Being Geniuses Together*, pp. 11-12; 39; 42.

But as usual, McAlmon soon grew restless; and he moved on to Paris.

McAlmon's most constant association with the literary figures of his time began in the spring of 1921 when Paris became a kind of base of operations for him. It was from here that he departed, and it was to Paris that he returned. He became an exceedingly well-known figure about town, so well known, in time, that he could be lampooned. In an "American Number" of *transition* (Summer, 1928), two of "Seven Occasional Poems" dealt with him. The first read:

WANTON PREJUDICE

I would rather live in Oregon and pack salmon
Than live in Nice and write like Robert McAlmon.[13]

Transition and *This Quarter*, rival literary quarterlies, were feuding at this time. Eliot Paul and Eugene Jolas of *transition* attempted to strike at their rival, Ernest Walsh, through one of the writers that *This Quarter* constantly championed. McAlmon was sufficiently controversial to serve their purposes. He had a local fame.

For some five years (1921-1926) McAlmon, sometimes with Bryher, sometimes alone, shuttled between London and Paris. Bryher had established residence in Swizerland in 1920, but McAlmon was rarely there. He made frequent trips to other parts of the continent, but the travel did not cure his general discontent. Though he said that he had come to Europe "because of events" and though he was certainly not romantic about "Old Europe" during these years, he preferred living in France to living anywhere else. In 1928 Eugene Jolas, by now sole editor of *transition,* inquired of several prominent expatriates concerning their residence abroad. Jolas's first question was: "Why do you prefer to live outside America?" McAlmon answered: "We, deracinated ones, if we are deracinated, may not all have come to Europe impelled by some motive of the heart and mind. I came, intending to return, or to travel much. I felt in America that Europe

---

[13] *Transition*, No. 13, p. 86. This couplet was published without attribution. In the next issue of *transition*, Slater Brown is revealed as the author of all seven of the verses. McAlmon was lampooned twice. The other reads:

After Heine
I dreamt that I was Pound himself,
Whom heavenly joy immerses,
And Ten McAlmons sat about
And praised my verses. (p. 86)

Brown's joke, though funny, is unjustified in fact. McAlmon, whatever else, was no sycophant; he was much too independent to flatter. In his autobiography he writes: ". . . while I mildly liked a poem or so of his [Pound's], I disliked his critical work generally." (p. 18)

was finished, decayed, war- and time-worn out. There it seemed that in Europe the sense of futility would be too enveloping. However, there is the rot of ripe fruit, and there is the blight and decay of green fruit.

"I. I prefer Europe, if you mean France, to America because there is less interference with private life here. There is interference, but to a foreigner, there is a fanciful freedom and grace of life not obtainable elsewhere. From various Frenchmen I gather that these statements do not apply to French citizens in a strong sense. It may be well to live in foreign countries; and to be definitely 'deracinated.' In that case the deficiencies of the land which accidentally gave us birth need disturb us no more than the legal, social, and human, infringements on our 'rights' bother us elsewhere. If by Europe you mean England, Italy, or Germany, I think America an exciting, stimulating, imaginative, country with the fresh imagination of youth and ignorance. . . ."[14] He denied that his age had a "revolutionary spirit either artistically or politically." McAlmon himself searched for a new world, but he did not think of himself as in revolt. As a matter of fact, he was simply recalcitrant.

Though he lived and worked in Paris, McAlmon never really deserted America. Though he spoke some French—he had polished up what he had learned in college—he associated almost exclusively with Americans. His books continued to be concerned with American problems. He clearly felt himself American. "I fail to discover fewer morons and bigotries in other countries than in the United States," he wrote later. "The other countries do not publicize their defectives so constantly."[15] In Europe the English-speaking expatriates among whom he lived were mostly writers. His observations of them illuminate their methods of composition and their habits of mind. They also tell us a good deal about the temper of the time.

When McAlmon went to Paris, James Joyce was finishing *Ulysses.* As usual he was having trouble finding a typist.[16] McAlmon was his constant drinking companion, and he called on him for help: "The husband of the English typist who was typing his work had destroyed some forty pages of the original script of *Ulysses,* because it was obscene. Joyce was naturally scared about handing work out to typists, and most typists would insist upon putting in punctuation which he did not desire. He knew that I typed not well, but quickly, and spoke suggestively of the point as we were drinking. I thought then, fifty pages, that's nothing, sure I'll type it for you.

---

[14] *transition,* No. 14 (Fall, 1928), pp. 98-99.
[15] *Being Geniuses Together,* p. 223.
[16] Cf. Herbert Gorman, *James Joyce* (New York, 1948), pp. 247-249.

"The next day he gave me the handwritten script, and his handwriting is minute and hen-scrawly; very difficult to decipher. With the script he gave me some four notebooks, and throughout the script were marks in red, yellow, blue, purple and green, referring me to phrases which must be inserted from one of the notebooks. For about three pages I was painstaking and actually re-typed one page to get the insertions in the right place. After that I thought 'Molly might just as well think this or that a page or two later or not at all,' and made the insertion wherever I happened to be typing. Years later upon asking Joyce if he'd noticed that I'd altered the mystic arrangement of Molloy's thought he said that he had, but agreed with my viewpoint. Molly's thoughts were irregular in several ways at best."[17]

According to McAlmon, Joyce was very modest. He sometimes doubted that readers would be permanently interested in *Ulysses,* and he told McAlmon so: "Now he declares that he is tired of hearing about *Ulysses.* There has been too much said about the book. When I suggest that perhaps in *Dubliners* there is writing of his much more apt to last he does not disagree and wonders also if he might not have developed that style of writing rather than going into words too entirely. It was his eye-sight, his inability to keep on reading freely, his incapacity to drink much without paying too great a price as regards his health, and his poverty, and the war, that decided many things which relate to his style and approach to writing. Nevertheless, his infatuation with words was born within him."[18]

Though McAlmon thought there was "too much said" about the book—perhaps *because* he thought so—he too engaged in an explication of one of Joyce's texts. His exegesis, entitled "Mr. Joyce Directs an Irish Prose Ballet," was published originally in *transition* and later republished in a volume called *An Exagmination of James Joyce.* It has had fairly wide distribution. McAlmon's account of the essay and Joyce's reaction to it underscore Joyce's constant irony: "Jolas [editor of *transition* at this time] was excited by an article on Joyce's *Work in Progress,* and kept muttering, 'Sensitive, very sensitive.' Having been urged to write the article by Sylvia Beach and Joyce, I read it to Joyce to see if he would mind it. The wily Mr. Joyce saw that all the 'he hopes he has done this or that,' 'he endeavours to' phrases were leg-pulling. Mr. Jolas, however, found it 'sensitive.' "[19]

[17] *Being Geniuses Together,* pp. 90-91. The episode is commented upon by Desmond MacCarthy, pp. 117-118.

[18] *Being Geniuses Together,* p. 251.

[19] *Being Geniuses Together,* p. 249. The essay appeared in *transition,* No. 15 (Febr., 1929), pp. 126-134, and was included in the volume (Paris, 1929). This book was distributed in the United States by New Directions, in England by Faber & Faber, both in 1929.

McAlmon's comments on other writers are also illuminating. He met Hemingway in 1922 in Rapallo where McAlmon had gone to see Ezra Pound. An anecdote of his, McAlmon says, suggested Hemingway's story "Hills Like White Elephants." Later he went to Spain with Hemingway, the first trip there for both of them.[20] Hemingway's reaction to an incident on the way to Madrid explains a good deal about both young men: "The next day, on the way to Madrid, our train stopped at a wayside station for a time. On the track beside us was a flat car, upon which lay the maggot-eaten corpse of a dog. I, feeling none too hale and hearty [because of a farewell party the night before], looked away, but Hemingway gave a dissertation on facing reality. It seemed that he had seen the stacked corpses of men maggot-eaten in the war in a similar way. He advised a detached and scientific attitude toward the corpse of the dog. He tenderly explained that we of our generation must inure ourselves to the sight of pain and grim reality. I recalled that Ezra Pound had talked once of Hemingway's 'self-hardening process.' At last he said, 'Hell, Mac, you write like a realist. Are you going to be a romantic on us?'

"I spurted forth some oath and went to the dining-car to order whisky. Not only was the sight of the dog before my eyes, its stench was in my nostrils, and I have seen many dead dogs, cats, and corpses borne in on the tide of New York harbour when working on a lumber barge. That dog had no distinction or novelty as a corpse. Several years later Paul Rosenfeld informed me that Hemingway had told this story to prove his assertion that I was a romanticist. He was realist enough himself to join me in the dining-car and have a whisky, however, but he surely had duly analyzed all of his sensations 'on seeing the maggot-eaten corpse of a dog on a flat car in Spain while wondering what it is that makes a guy who has seen as much of life as McAlmon shudder.' "[21] When, later, McAlmon told Williams of this incident, Williams "thoroughly approved" of Hemingway's actions.[22]

McAlmon was a hard one to impress, and very few did. He prided himself on seeing through sham, and he constantly tried to test what he read against his own experience. Like others of his generation, he

---

[20] The account of the origins of the story is in *Being Geniuses Together*, p. 159. Hemingway wrote two naughty pieces for *Das Querschnittbuch* (Berlin, 1924) entitled, "The Soul of Spain with McAlmon and Bird the Publishers," pp. 229-230; 278. These pieces are in the manner of Gertrude Stein. The first begins:

> In the rain in the rain in the rain in the rain in Spain.
> Does it rain in Spain?
> Oh yes my dear on the contrary and there are no bull fights.

[21] *Being Geniuses Together*, pp. 160-161.

[22] *Autobiography*, p. 212.

was not a man of faith. His comments on the stories of Hemingway give a fair indication of the tack he constantly took, and they are perceptive enough to be of continuing interest: "It is difficult to say who started the attitude in writing which occurs in *My Old Man* and much present American work. It is not so much a style or an approach as an emotional attitude; that of an older person who insists upon trying to think and write as a child, and children in my experience are much colder and more ruthless in their observations than the child characters, be they of child-age or old men, in this type of writing. . . . Hemingway, and a number of others have written in that, to me, falsely-naive manner. They may write of gangsters, prizefighters, bull-fighters, or children, but the hurt-child-being-brave tone is there, and all conversation is reduced to lone words or staccato phrases. . . . I read with an incredulous eye when reviewers comment much about this or that writer's ability to capture the 'inflection' and 'intonation' of American types and the American language."[23]

From the time of his marriage in 1921 until 1923, McAlmon traveled. He wrote constantly, of his life on the plains, in college and in Greenwich Village. He describes and defends his hard-drinking and gregarious life on the Left Bank in an essay on the celebration of Bastille Day in "Truer than Most Accounts." He tells how he drank all night with his friends and, after sleep, drank again. In Paris, he wrote, "People soon find their level, and it may be those who find their level is very middle or lowdown, who return to their native countries to condemn Paris. They could have found thugs, bootleggers, diseased beings, vicious degenerates, and futile people in America in any village or city they choose to visit. They could not, however, find so large a program of entertainment in these villages and towns." McAlmon constantly "migrated"—his word—to escape boredom. He tried to keep interested. He needed evidence of life about him. England he thought did not know how to live, and, "frightened, it dares not experiment. Thanks to the younger generation of America, America will learn. It, like the artists in the Quarter, will come through if it means to."[24] But now, since he wanted life, McAlmon remained in Europe.

He also worked. In 1922 in Paris he established the Contact Publishing Company. That is, he hired Maurice Darantière of Dijon to print the first of his books, a collection of sketches and stories called *A Hasty Bunch.* Darantière had printed *Ulysses* for Sylvia Beach, and

[23] *Being Geniuses Together,* pp. 156-157.
[24] *The Exile,* 2 (Autumn, 1927), 40-86. The quotations are from the concluding paragraph, pp. 85-86.

he was to do almost all of McAlmon's printing. Within a year McAlmon and William Bird had joined publishing forces. Bird was an American newspaperman working in Paris. Their association worked very well for some three years. Altogether Contact Editions and the Three Mountains Press brought out some thirty titles.[25]

A great deal of McAlmon's energy was used up by this publishing, by his continual travel, and by the emotional turmoil resulting from his marriage. Even though his interest in writing and writers continued, he could not seem to find anything that required his permanent and complete allegiance. He tried his hand at philanthropy. Using his connections with the Ellerman fortune, he attempted to help struggling artists. At one time he was able to interest Lady Ellerman in Wyndham Lewis; and at another time she agreed to subsidize George Antheil, the composer, for two years.[26] McAlmon helped others out of his own pocket. After Emanuel Carnevali returned to Italy ill in 1921, McAlmon supplied him with a monthly allowance, perhaps for as long as four years.[27] Whenever Pound had a scheme for subsidizing deserving poets, he turned to McAlmon as a matter of course. McAlmon's friends remember that he was generous to a fault. The money McAlmon used, strictly speaking, may not always have been his, but nobody doubted that he came by it honestly and that he exchanged full measure for it. And he was no more generous with Sir John's ample fortune than he was with his own meager earnings, even the money he had earned laboring in the New York harbor.

And then, in 1926, McAlmon and Bryher separated, and in 1927 they were divorced. Though Bryher promptly remarried, it was on McAlmon's suggestions that the marriage was dissolved. McAlmon makes only one comment on the divorce in his autobiography: "Incidentally it was my suggestion that I felt my marriage was not a go. It represented to me more things that I did NOT want in life than I could cope with."[28] McAlmon went to America; and Bryher and her new husband, Kenneth Macpherson, founded a new publishing company. The "new publishing house," called "Pool," in July, 1927, issued the first number of *Close-up*, a high-brow review of the cinematic art which was to have a distinguished history. Pool also brought out several books. The Macphersons made Switzerland their home base.

---

[25] A full account of the publishing activities of Bird and McAlmon is given below, Section III, McAlmon's Publishing.
[26] *Being Geniuses Together*, p. 93.
[27] Pound, *Letters*, p. 222.
[28] *Being Geniuses Together*, p. 224.

McAlmon in the meantime had sailed for Los Angeles, to see his mother; and one of his best stories, "Machine-Age Romance," grew out of his experience on board ship. Though he had come halfway around the world, he did not remain long in California. Very shortly dissatisfied, he went back to New York, stopping for a time at the now famous art center of Taos, New Mexico. Soon he returned to Paris. But he did not stay in Paris either, though he continued his publishing activities from there for another year or so. On the Riviera, where he spent considerable time, he met Edwin M. Lanham and encouraged him to write his memories of the sea. Published by McAlmon as *Sailors Don't Care* (1929), the book was subsequently rewritten and republished in the United States.

In spite of his interest in writing and publishing, McAlmon now seemed more at a loss than ever; and late in 1929, he returned to the United States on his way to Mexico. "Rumors about a vital art movement and group in Mexico City had been drifting about for several years and friends of mine were in Mexico City," he wrote.[29] In spite of the "group," Mexico too turned out to be disappointing, or, rather, not permanently interesting. After a time McAlmon went to an out-of-the-way village in the West, where he remained for several months. Some of his best autobiographical fiction was written of his experiences there. Pretty badly butchered when it appeared in the revived *Contact* (1932), "Mexican Interval" was printed entire in *The Indefinite Huntress and Other Stories* (1932). Its conclusion is significant of McAlmon's recurring attitude toward the places he lived in and the world about him: "Suddenly I realize that my stay here has been a vacation of variation only; it has not been release, and I don't want to escape from the world I knew before."[30] Here pretty explicitly McAlmon shows both sides of his nature: his desire for "release" and, simultaneously, his desire for stability. If this irresoluble conflict is in all of us, it is not so strong, perhaps, as it was in McAlmon.

He headed back toward New York City and Greenwich Village, stopping off in Albuquerque, New Mexico, where Norman Macleod was bringing out *The Morado*, a literary quarterly. The quarterly lasted only four or five issues; by the time it had disappeared, McAlmon had departed for the north. In 1930 and 1931 Greenwich Village was like a suburb of Paris, and McAlmon found many of his old friends and drinking companions there. William Carlos Williams was not far away, in Rutherford, New Jersey; and Zukovsky and his "Objectivists" were active. McAlmon saw something of them. When

---

[29] *Being Geniuses Together,* p. 305.
[30] (Paris, 1932), p. 144.

Zukovsky published *An "Objectivists" Anthology* in 1932, he included poems by McAlmon.[31] While he was in New York, two booksellers, David Moss and Martin Kamin, attempted to persuade him to edit a magazine that their bookstore in the Barbizon-Plaza could support. Their plans failed to materialize, for McAlmon's backers were not interested in the kind of inclusive review that he proposed. He thought that the exclusively literary review was passé, at least for a time, since the depression was increasing general awareness of the importance of political and economic problems. At this time (1932) his name appeared on the masthead of the revived *Contact,* but he had no editorial association with it.

Moss and Kamin had other plans for McAlmon, but these also fell through. Their bookshop had come into the possession of a number of Contact Editions—Three Mountains Press books, and they offered them for sale in New York at prices considerably higher than Bird and McAlmon had originally asked for them. It is difficult to guess how these books found their way into their shop, for McAlmon had always had considerable difficulty getting what he published into the United States. Moss and Kamin proposed in 1932 that Contact Editions be continued from their bookstores, with McAlmon as editor. Though momentarily tempted, McAlmon finally refused the job and returned to Europe. He had nothing whatever to do with the only book published by Contact Editions in New York. It was Nathanael West's somewhat adolescent *The Dream Life of Balso Snell.*

The first four years of the Thirties were productive for McAlmon. Though he continued, rootless, to wander, he now published some of his best fiction. He wrote his autobiography, *Being Geniuses Together,* and when New Directions brought out a volume of his poems in 1937, the only volume of his ever published in his native country, he included some verse written during this period. The volume was called, rather significantly, *Not Alone Lost.* During this period, McAlmon was living intemperately, at a greater pace perhaps than ever before. "And what iz gone wrong with McAlmon. The kid just playin' the fool, or whatever?" Pound writes to a mutual friend. ". . . I hope he ain't gone plumb to hell."[32]

By 1935, McAlmon's literary life was nearly complete. Aside from a few poems printed in a few little magazines, he wrote nothing more. Wandering and living hard, he was of considerable concern to his old friends. The war found him still in France. He did not return

---

[31] (Le Beausset, Var, France & New York, 1932).
[32] *Letters,* p. 266. It is said that New Directions brought out McAlmon's volume of verse only on Dr. William's insistence.

finally to the United States until 1946 when he went to El Paso. There he worked for his brothers in a surgical supply house. Having contracted tuberculosis as early as 1940, in the Fifties he went to the deserts of the Southwest. He died there, in the desert, in February, 1956. It is said that he was discouraged and embittered at the last.

McAlmon was without doubt a phenomenon of his time. Separated from the ties of place and society, he set out to find his own way, rejecting conventional help. He had a kind of Rimbaud career, as one of his friends has said. Too impatient for long-range planning, incapable of developing a pattern of action over a period of time, he seemed consumed by the very energy that nourished him. "Williams has said that I have a 'genius for life,'" he wrote, "while bemoaning his New England soul and his not having ventured far or long from the town of his birth. He may be right about me; if despair, a capacity for indifference, long and heavy spells of ennui which takes bottles of strong drink to cure, and a gregarious but not altogether loving nature, is a 'genius for life,' I have it."[33]

McAlmon's friends talk of his misdirected talent, how he was "potentially a greatly talented writer." But he was prodigal with himself, his money, his abilities; and he was overly generous, saving nothing for himself. He ended with almost nothing. Constitutionally unable to accept help or direction from anyone, he died in the desert, as he had lived, alone. And all his friends, now far away, could give no aid.

[33] *Being Geniuses Together,* p. 184.

McAlmon's Publishing

When McAlmon lived in Greenwich Village, he edited and published with Williams *Contact,* a small literary periodical; and when he got to Paris, he founded the Contact Publishing Company and brought out a number of volumes of avant-garde poetry and fiction. His actions as a publisher and editor were appropriate to his time; they would have been impossible before World War I, and similar activities have probably become unnecessary since World War II. Just as there is nowhere an account of McAlmon's life, there is no account of his publishing. Though I cannot give here a history of the influence of publishing houses on the literature of the Twentieth Century—a job which needs doing—I can at least explain McAlmon's not insignificant part in the publishing of his time. I want first to consider *Contact,* his magazine.

THE MAGAZINE

During the time of McAlmon's literary activity, publication for the "new" writer was often difficult. James Joyce, William Carlos Williams, Marianne Moore, Gertrude Stein and others could not easily find businessmen willing to accept their work, for their books were almost certain to be financial losses or scandals or both. As a consequence the writers of the time turned to publication in periodicals, hoping that they might through this medium find or create an audience.

Of course the great commercial magazines, like the great commercial publishers, were closed to these new writers. *Harper's, Scribner's,* the *Atlantic,* all were firmly in the hands of the old guard; and very properly, since general readers and advertisers demanded the New England tradition. In order to get their work into print, the new writers founded their own magazines. In some cases these periodicals brought their contributors to the attention of appropriate people: other writers, occasional publishers, a few readers. *Poetry, A Magazine of Verse,* founded by Harriet Monroe in Chicago in 1912, was probably the most important of these periodicals; and it, almost alone, survives to this day. In England in the same World War I period, for a few years *The Egoist* received the new writers; and *The New Review* (1914-1929) in both America and Europe printed new prose and poetry. Through its championing of *Ulysses,* if for nothing else, it achieved considerable fame. After 1920 a number of important periodicals turned up. Probably the most significant in England was T. S. Eliot's *The Criterion* (1922-1939); the most important in America were *The Dial,* edited by Scofield Thayer and Marianne Moore (1920-1929), and *The Hound and Horn,* a smug and pontifical "Harvard Miscellany" (1927-1934). These periodicals and their kind were important stopgaps, for they gave the experimental writer a chance to be heard by people who might be persuaded to listen.[1]

McAlmon founded and edited such a magazine, called *Contact.* It had five issues between December, 1920 and June, 1923. The first four appeared in the first six months after its founding, and the fifth some two years later. *Contact* was an important spokesman for the point of view which William Carlos Williams represents; but the periodical, Williams says in his autobiography, was primarily McAlmon's. He was its "instigator," and with some help from Williams, he supported it.[2] After the fourth issue, McAlmon left New York with his wife, and the magazine suspended publication until June, 1923. Then one more issue appeared. *Contact* was revived in 1932, but McAlmon had no part in it at this time.

Like most of the "little magazines," this one subsisted on a tight budget. The first, second and fourth issues, (December, 1920, January, 1921, and the "Advertising Number" [Summer, 1921]), were mimeographed on brief size paper. The third number [Spring, 1921] was printed and contained a number of pictures. They were black and white reproductions of paintings by Rex Slinkard whose posthumous diary Williams and McAlmon had been publishing in the paper. The fifth and final issue, June, 1923, was printed. No issue was longer than nineteen pages, three of them being twelve pages or shorter. Considering its brevity and its tenuous hold on life, it is remarkable that its literary quality was as high as indeed it was. "There was some good stuff lying around," Williams wrote later, and *Contact* "printed it; direct, uncompromising writing."[3]

---

[1] The whole subject of the literary periodical in the Twentieth Century has been treated exhaustively by Frederick J. Hoffman, Charles Allen and Carolyn F. Ulrich, *The Little Magazine: A History and a Bibliography* (Princeton, 1947).

[2] See Williams, *Autobiography,* pp. 175-176.

[3] *Autobiography,* p. 175.

Though Williams and McAlmon saw themselves revolting against the dead hand of Longfellow, Whittier and the *Atlantic Monthly,* they also saw themselves as counter-revolutionaries, revolting against the new attitudes that T. S. Eliot represented. In the first issue of *Contact* the editors explain their choice of name. Good writing, they say, established "the essential contact between words and the locality that breeds them, in this case America. . . ." McAlmon probably wrote the magazine's initial "Manifesto." He says that "that art which attains is indigenous of experience and relations, and the artist works to express perceptions rather than to attain standards of achievement." Through all the issues Williams and McAlmon repeat their central contention, that the perception of immediate reality must take precedence over traditional literary requirements. "An artist's prime occupation is with life. Art is his outlet." McAlmon had written a few months before in *The Little Review*: "One does not become an artist by going into the arts. One has some perception, some interpretation, some essential record that one must leave."[4] Williams wrote later: "Critically Eliot returned us to the classroom just at the moment when I felt that we were on the point of an escape to matters much closer to the essence of a new art form itself—rooted in the locality which should give it fruit."[5] McAlmon and he insisted on the importance of first-hand experience, not that vicarious experience which could be learned from books.

The material in *Contact* has stood the test of time remarkably well; the editors had notable critical acumen. The first issue was the least interesting, though it contained some poems and prose by Wallace Gould, Marsden Hartley and Mina Loy. Hartley, the poet-painter, and Gould, the poet, both wrote a variety of vers libre; Mina Loy, an English lady now a part of the Greenwich Village group, had had some of her very cerebral poetry included in Kreymborg's *Others*.[6] In subsequent issues were poems by Marianne Moore, "Those Various Scalpels" and "In the Days of Prismatic Color," which have since been printed in her *Collected Poems;* and four poems by Wallace Stevens, two of which, "Invective against Swans" and "Infanta Marina," have become celebrated. The magazine contained work by H. D. and Bryher, an essay by Kenneth Burke dealing with Laforgue, and, in the last issue, poems by John Rodker, Kay Boyle and Glenway Wescott. The editors also published a long book review by Marianne

---

[4] "Essentials," VII, 3 (Sept.-Dec., 1920), p. 69.
[5] *Autobiography,* p. 174.
[6] Ezra Pound comments on Mina Loy in a review of her work which was reprinted in *The Little Review Anthology,* Margaret Anderson, ed., (New York, 1953), pp. 188-189.

Moore, and a short one by Ezra Pound. A good deal of Williams's own work and some of McAlmon's was included. Though McAlmon's work was not of remarkably high quality, it was included in his volume *Explorations* (1921). Williams printed some of his more celebrated pieces, like "Portrait of the Artist," and some critical work of considerable interest. He also published a very funny auto-biographical bit about a mad baroness-poet. This same baroness, incidentally, appears prominently in Margaret Anderson's memoirs and in other contemporary reminiscences.

Not all of *Contact* was deadly serious. It had its share of eccentricity. The letters of Rex Slinkard, for example, are an un-affected record of a young man's initial responses to the world about him, but from this distance they hardly deserve the prominence they received. In the second number McAlmon published a piece by one Virgil Jordan which is pretty erotic. When Hart Crane saw this issue, he praised the poems of Wallace Stevens and the "talk" of Dr. Williams, but he was revolted by the selection by Virgil Jordan.[7] The jolliest issue of the five was number four, the "advertising number." It contained announcements that "writings" similar to those contained therein "are for sale at prices fixed by the author." Williams offers "sample poems," a "sample prose piece" and a "sample critical statement." The next issue of *Contact* does not record any rush for the writer's wares.

All the issues of *Contact* reflect an attractive youthful exuberance and insouciance. The reader can imagine the delight with which the numbers were put together, but they attracted no buyers. By 1932 when *Contact* was revived, McAlmon's confidence in the value of the experimental magazine was severely shaken. "After many years," he wrote, "I decided that they did not help the working artist to arrive; and they are quite as apt to create antagonism on the part of publishers and in the minds of certain people who insist upon seeing all their contributors as a school, and therefore, precious boys and girls."[8] Williams has never lost faith in these litle magazines, however; and in the 1932 *Contact,* he published the beginning of a bibliography of them by David Moss. Williams has said that he regards all the quarterlies as issues of the same venture, changing their places of

---

[7] His comment on the magazine appears in a letter to Gorham Munson, dated 2/11/21; see *The Letters of Hart Crane, 1916-1932*, Brom Weber, ed., (New York, 1952), p. 53. Crane links Virgil Jordan and McAlmon without obvious cause. Later, in a letter to Munson dated Febr. 22, 1922, pp. 79-80, Crane commends Munson for his "nicely administered spanking of McAlmon" in a recent issue of *Gargoyle.*

[8] *Being Geniuses Together,* p. 319.

publication as the men and women who write for them move about.[9] When one looks through these experimental journals, one cannot help being struck how often they are sounding boards for the accepted writers of a later generation and how regularly they contain the same contributors. A good many of these writers, including Williams himself, would have had no publisher without these fly-by-night periodicals. One must conclude that McAlmon's disillusionment is based more on his own ill fortune than on a general consideration of the course of American letters in his time. At any rate, when he got to Europe, he attempted publishing on a grander scale, and he became a much more important figure in the literary world.

THE BOOKS

Though the writers of McAlmon's generation frequently had trouble getting a hearing, the possibilities of publication for unconventional writers had improved a good deal during the first two decades of the Twentieth Century. By 1914 it was clear that a shift in taste and literary forms was under way. As a result between 1890 and 1915 the literary and publishing center of the country moved from Boston to New York. The change marks the death of the New England tradition. "At one time," one of the prominent American publishers has said, "there was a saying current in the [book] trade that if the books on the list of Houghton, Mifflin & Co., of Boston should vanish little American literature would remain; for this great house published Emerson, Longfellow, Hawthorne, Whittier, Lowell, Aldrich and other leaders of the time."[10] Before 1890 Boston, though publishing the American classics, had often seemed little more than an outpost of London, in matters of taste and business alike. The Victorian masters were the standard by which all writing was measured, and they were imported already printed. They were distributed by American branches of English firms, and they formed the backbone of the "genteel tradition." It was against this tradition that the new generation revolted.

Writers who wished to be published by the old houses—that is, writers who wished to be published at all—had to be willing to be judged by those who endorsed Longfellow and Tennyson. This state

[9] *Autobiography*, p. 266.
[10] Frederick A. Stokes, "A Publisher's Random Notes—1880-1935," *The Bowker Lectures on Book Publishing, First Series* (New York, 1943), p. 33. Theodore Dreiser has given an account of his difficulties in getting his revolutionary *Sister Carrie* published in the years just following the turn of the century. The account is to be found in *The Colophon, A Book Collectors' Quarterly,* Part V (New York, 1931) [unpaged].

of affairs could hardly encourage "new writing." When new publishing houses sprang up about 1915, houses that were to give the avant-garde at least a hearing, they appeared significantly in New York. The provincial New York of Henry James's youth and Edith Wharton's novels was disappearing by 1910, under the impetus of masses of immigrants; and by 1914 New York had become the international metropolis that it remains. Three important houses, reflecting the wider tastes of an international city, were founded before 1920. B. W. Heubsch, Alfred Knopf and Horace Liveright brought to American attention much new European writing which had not, formerly, been available. As publishing took on an international flavor, it became increasingly hospitable to native experimental writing. Even so the "advanced" writer felt isolated, and he still had trouble finding a publisher.

Alfred A. Knopf was the leader of the new publishers. When he was with Doubleday, Page, an old and established firm, he had 'discovered" Conrad who had been lost in the book lists. He promoted him into a best-seller. For a brief period, Knopf subsequently had sold books for Mitchell Kennerley. Kennerley, one of the colorful figures of Twentieth Century publishing, had come to America from England in 1905, and for a time cut quite a swath. By 1915 he had published Van Wyck Brooks, Samuel Butler, George Moore, Frank Harris, Vachel Lindsay, Walter Lippman and D. H. Lawrence. He did not remain an influence, however; by 1920 his authors had gone to other houses and his books were scattered.

Knopf founded the house that bears his name in 1915, and by 1920 he was already publishing distinguished writers, many of them Europeans.[11] Ten of his first eleven books were translations, and in 1917 fifty-three of his seventy-seven books were by foreigners. To a generation brought up on Henry Van Dyke and the Boston Brahmins, his importations must have seemed exotic indeed. By 1920 he had published, some for the first time in America, books by Thomas Mann, Vicente Blasco Ibáñez, Leo Tolstoi, Arthur Waley's versions of the Chinese, and Shalem Aleichem. Moreover, Knopf was relatively hospitable to new American and British writers. In addition to such safe (and profitable) figures as Willa Cather and E. M. Forster, he sponsored Maxwell Bodenheim and T. S. Eliot (both in 1920), Wyndham Lewis and Ezra Pound. In 1916 and 1917 he commissioned Alfred Kreymborg to edit his two famous anthologies of contemporary verse, *Others.*

[11] There is an informative "Profile" of Knopf in *The New Yorker,* XXIV (Nov. 20, 1948), pp. 44-56; (Nov. 27, 1948), pp. 36-52; (Dec. 4, 1948), pp. 40-47.

B. H. Huebsch and Horace Liveright also tried to be generous with new writers. Huebsch brought out Sherwood Anderson, and continued to publish his books, in spite of the criticism they received.[12] By 1920 Huebsch had published Van Wyck Brooks, Joyce, Lawrence and Thorstein Veblen. Liveright (Boni and Liveright by 1920) in the meantime had published O'Neill, a couple volumes of Pound's, E. E. Cummings's *The Enormous Room,* T. S. Eliot's *The Waste Land,* Lewis Mumford's *The Story of Utopias* and a volume by Djuna Barnes. Although Huebsch's and Liveright's lists may have been less impressive than Knopf's, they were distinguished; and they contained a good number of advanced English and American writers.

In 1919 a fourth important house was founded. Alfred Harcourt, who formerly had been associated with Henry Holt, and his friend Donald Brace established Harcourt, Brace and Howe; in 1920 the firm became Harcourt, Brace and Company. When it was formed, Harcourt took several of Holt's first names with him to the new firm: Walter Lippman, J. E. Spingarn, Louis Untermeyer, Harold J. Laski. The new firm made a spectacular start with Sinclair Lewis's *Main Street* and Keynes's *Economic Consequences of the Peace,* and by 1923 it had published all the "Bloomsbury Group"—Clive Bell, the Woolfs, Lytton Strachey, E. M. Forster and others—as well as important American and European figures like Carl Becker, Heywood Broun, Jung, Wittgenstein, Heinrich Mann. Harcourt, Brace was a worthy colleague of Huebsch, Liveright and Knopf. In 1927 Bennett Cerf, a vice president with Liveright, took over the Modern Library and founded Random House. Cerf has also been hospitable to new writers, but by the time he arrived, many of them had won a place for themselves. All five of these publishing houses continued to welcome unknown writers. In time they were joined by some of the older publishers.[13]

Perhaps more interesting than these, however, are the fly-by-night publishing ventures, the little commercial houses which tried their hands at literary publication. They have an important place in any account of the literary publication of this century. They ought not be passed over. Two are typical and interesting: the Four Seas Company of Boston which existed from 1913 until it was absorbed by

---

[12] See, for example, Sherwood Anderson, *Memoirs* (New York, 1942), especially "Waiting for Ben Heubsch," pp. 283-292, and "Meeting Horace Liveright," pp. 351-355. Anderson gives a spirited account of one new writer's dealings with publishers.

[13] A readable account of some of the problems of modern book publishing from the point of view of the publishers can be found in *The Bowker Lectures on Book Publishing.* A businesslike account is to be found in Hellmut Lehmann-Haupt, *The Book in America: A History of the Making, the Selling, and the Collecting of Books in the United States* (New York, 1939).

Bruce Humphries, Inc., also of Boston, in 1930; and the Macaulay Company which lasted a few years longer. What happened to them is what happened to other little presses that attempted to publish avant-garde works.

In the first years of its existence The Four Seas Company specialized in the wholesome, the uplifting and the educational. In 1913 it had on its lists *School Ethics* by Eleanor Marchbanks and *Running and Training* by the coach of the Harvard track team. By 1915 the house offered *Bars Between* by Mary M. Dean, a "clean wholesome story," and *Manna for the Months* by Helen Elizabeth Jeffers, "a series of original thoughts for mental, physical and spiritual progress." When founded, the company had been financed out of thin air, for it was started with one hundred dollars of borrowed money and did its own printing. Edmund R. Brown, the editor, had been New England representative of Kennerley and Knopf, and in 1917 began publishing books of a literary nature, by his friends and their friends. In one year he added to his lists books by Conrad Aiken, Richard Aldington, Gordon Bottomly, Grace Coolidge, Lord Dunsany, John Gould Fletcher and William Carlos Williams. By 1920 he offered in addition, in an "International Pocket Library" at twenty-five cents, Hardy, Tagore, Ibáñez and stories from the Russian; and in a "Contemporary Series," Sardou, Gorki, Merivale, Hofsmannsthal, Jacinto Benevento and others. By 1920 two books by Williams appeared: *Kora in Hell* and *The Tempers*. There were no significant additions to this list in the Twenties, and a good number of these sold very badly indeed. In 1930 The Four Sea Company was taken over by Bruce Humphries, which continued its inexpensive "International Pocket Library." Edmund R. Brown has remained with Bruce Humphries to this day.[14]

The Macaulay Company of New York had a more spectacular change of direction. Originally a publisher of "romances," it advertised novels like *A Lady of New Orleans*: "Hers was the fault of loving well, but not wisely," and F. Hugh Herbert's novel, *There You Are*, in which "Joan insisted upon being kissed." One of the more interesting titles is by Fulton Oursler, the same Oursler who has become celebrated for his religious books. It is a novel, *Sandalwood*: "Before your eyes Fulton Oursler holds up to view the secret that nearly every

[14] Brown, in association with Edward J. O'Brien, the short-story anthologist, and William Stanley Braithwaite, a prominent critic and anthologist of the time, had also founded a poetry journal (in 1912) and planned to call it "Poetry." When Harriet Monroe of Chicago received a circular announcing it, she wrote to Boston indignantly, accusing Brown and the others of "stealing her idea and name." The Boston group quickly changed their periodical to "The Poetry Journal." Subsequently Miss Monroe was very friendly.

married man fatuously thinks is his alone—the fact that at some time he has been untrue to his wife in thought, if not in deed." The Macaulay Company also carried a full line of Elinor Glyn, at seventy-five cents per copy.

And then in 1927 Matthew Josephson became editor-in-chief, and the company changed direction. In addition to Elinor Glyn and Fulton Oursler, Macaulay published a Stark Young translation of Machiavelli's *Mandragola*, and the first of several *American Caravans*, edited by Van Wyck Brooks (who subsequently withdrew), Alfred Kreymborg, Lewis Mumford, and Paul Rosenfeld. In 1928 Josephson brought out his own *Zola and His Times;* Dos Passos's *Airways, Inc.;* Williams's *A Voyage to Pagany;* and Wallace Gould's *Aphrodite.* Subsequently Ford Madox Ford's *No Enemy* and a number of avant-garde works appeared. In 1930 *Whither Whither or After Sex What?* was published; Kenneth Burke, E. E. Cummings, Robert M. Coates, James Thurber, E. B. White, Malcolm Cowley, Edmund Wilson and others contributed to it. But the house ran into difficulty. By 1932 it returned to such novels as *The Reluctant Virgin;* by 1937 it had ceased to exist.

But even though these publishers accepted and promoted much writing that would have been unacceptable not half a generation earlier, many new writers, some of acknowledged merit, could not find publishers in the United States. It is significant that a number of Americans had to leave home to reach their first fame. When Robert Frost went to England in 1912, for example, he had been unable to find a publisher in the United States. But when David Nutt of London published *A Boy's Will* in 1913 and *North of Boston* in 1914, he quickly achieved a certain fame. After he was accepted abroad he was welcomed in America. T. S. Eliot similarly appeared first in England, almost privately. His first volume, *Prufrock and Other Observations,* was brought out by the Egoist Press in 1917, his *Poems* by Leonard and Virginia Woolf's private Hogarth Press in 1919. Knopf produced the first American edition of his poems, in 1920. Ezra Pound also made his name abroad. "My American publishers do not exist," he wrote R. P. Blackmur in 1924. "It becomes more and more evident that the American publisher must be left out of one's calculations. Likewise English and henglish publishers."[15] He exaggerates the plight of the young writer, of course, for publication was not as impossible as he habitually makes out. But still the road to publication for the group of new writers to which McAlmon belonged was by no means easy. If it is true that every new writer must create his own

[15] Pound, *Letters,* p. 190.

audience, one is forced to say that American publishers at this time were often unwilling to carry a writer and publicize his work until it had had a chance to develop a community of readers.

Even before McAlmon's appearance as a publisher, the new writers had found publishers among themselves. These publishers may not have been as hospitable as McAlmon, but some were more businesslike. The most famous were Albert and Charles Boni. Before World War I, the Boni brothers were proprietors of the Washington Square Bookshop, but by 1914 they had graduated from book selling to book publishing, moving from Greenwich Village into the world at large. By 1917 they had gone into partnership with Horace Liveright, that inspired wild man of publishing, and with him had founded Boni and Liveright. Though the firm retained both names until 1928, the Bonis early ceased to have a voice in the firm. Other booksellers in the early World War I period tried their hands at publishing too. Frank Shay, for example, published Edna St. Vincent Millay's poetry when she lived in Waverly Place and acted with the Provincetown Players.[16]

In Chicago somewhat later the Covici-McGee bookshop in West Washington Street, hangout for Ben Hecht, Maxwell Bodenheim and other Chicago writers, began issuing books. By 1924 Covici had separated from McGee who, after going into partnership with a man named Hyman, quickly (1926) went out of business. Pascal Covici had a distinguished career. First known as Pascal Covici, Publisher, his house became Covici, Friede and remained active until 1939. Though this house had a New York office, it remained principally a Chicago firm, befriending such people as Margaret Anderson of *The Little Review*, Ben Hecht, Arthur Machen and Samuel Putnam. Covici published three of the four issues of Ezra Pound's quarterly, *The Exile* (1927-28), which were edited in Italy because, as Pound says, "the behavior of a customs department plus the state of our copyright laws are such that but for Mr. Covici undertaking to print this second issue, the editors would have desisted." Pound continues in the same vein: "Why the United States has a copyright law designed chiefly to encourage theft, I am unable to say.

"As to Mr. Coolidge's economic policy, I have one further suggestion—namely, that he can completely eliminate the cost of lunatic asylums by dressing the present inmates in customs uniforms and placing them in ports and along the frontiers. This will dispense with

---

[16] A rather unsympathetic account of the literary revolution is to be found in Albert Parry, *Garrets and Pretenders* (New York, 1933).

the present employees entirely and the public will be just as well served."[17]

One must not overstate the case against commercial publishers. A great deal of the writing that had difficulty finding a place was not worthy of much attention; and most first-rate writers, after a first promising book, were quickly promoted by the big houses. Hemingway, for instance, after his first two volumes, was accepted, first by Liveright, later by Scribner's. McAlmon and Pound complained, however, that publishers generally would not take a *first* risk: Hemingway found an American publisher only *after* McAlmon and Bird had printed his first books. Clearly the problem for a beginning writer was in finding a first publisher.

When McAlmon became associated with writers in Paris, he saw, as he had seen in Greenwich Village earlier, that most of them had difficulty getting an early hearing. He saw, moreover, that writers had a chance of catching a commercial publisher's eye once their work was in print. In Paris his Contact Publishing Company was founded to print these early books so that their authors might have an opening wedge. This publishing company was a kind of showcase for the talents of the expatriates, and a significant number of the books McAlmon brought out got American publishers for their authors. In this sense the Contact Publishing Company was a kind of pump-primer.

It was a pump-primer in another sense too. By printing the work of young writers, McAlmon encouraged the creation of new work. When he printed "promising" work, he brought the young writers that he sponsored one step closer to writing of mature achievement. If new writers were assured of a hearing, they might proceed to further developments and greater accomplishment. A great publishing house could not afford to take chances on the "promising" writers that McAlmon's private press undertook as a matter of course.

McAlmon's general observations in advertisements on his aims in publishing give a fair indication of his attitude toward Contact Editions, but they do not explain what he was trying to accomplish. McAlmon was not one given to great announcements of high purpose. In the first issue of *the transatlantic review*, McAlmon wrote: "At intervals of two weeks to six months, or six years, we will bring out books by various writers who seem not likely to be published by other publishers, for commercial or legislative reasons." After a partial list of his books then available, the advertisement concludes: "Three hundred only of each book will be printed. These books are pub-

[17] *The Exile*, 2 (Autumn, 1927), p. 120.

lished simply because they are written, and we like them well enough to get them out."[18] In a more formal "general statement," McAlmon writes: "Contact Editions are not concerned with what the 'public' wants. There are commercial publishers who *know* the public and its tastes. If books seem to us to have something of individuality, intelligence, talent, a live sense of literature, and a quality which has the odour and timbre of authenticity, we publish them. We admit that eccentricities exist."[19] When, in 1932, it looked as though Contact Editions would be continued from New York, this general statement was reasserted substantially unchanged.[20] In these statements McAlmon is trying to apply his fierce independence to business. He was too impatient to put down in a fuller statement what he hoped in his less cynical and less off-hand moments to accomplish.

The Contact Publishing Company achieved considerable success both in bringing unknown writers to the attention of commercial publishers and in encouraging new writing. The first books produced were volumes of stories by McAlmon himself. In 1922 or 1923, Maurice Darantière of Dijon printed a small edition of his *A Hasty Bunch,* and it had almost no distribution.[21] Undated, without place of publication or publisher, like all of McAlmon's books it was a handsome little paper-backed volume on good paper with clear print and generous margins. Also like all of McAlmon's books, it was not carefully proofread.

The next two books that McAlmon published, his *A Companion Volume* and *Post-Adolescence,* also did not bear dates; but Bryher's *Two Selves,* the book that followed these two, is dated 1923. Until this time these publishing activities were financed by McAlmon out of his own pocket, from the allowances to him and Bryher from Sir John Ellerman. Printing was very cheap in France, of course, and these four paper-covered books could not have been a great drain on

---

[18] I, i (Jan., 1924), inside back cover.

[19] Quoted in Will Ransom, *Private Presses and Their Books* (New York, 1929), p. 432. Ransom's entry for the Three Mountains Press is inaccurate. Neither Theron Cooper nor J. Krebs Friend, who was associated with *the transatlantic review,* had anything to do with the press; both are erroneously listed as joint proprietors with Bird.

[20] See the advertisement for Contact Editions (Three Mountains Press) in *Contact* I, i (Febr., 1932), p. 3.

[21] Emanuel Carnevali speaks of *A Hasty Bunch* in a review of *Explorations,* McAlmon's first volume of poems, in *Poetry,* XX (1922), pp. 155-157. William Bird, McAlmon's partner in publishing, says in a personal letter that the volume was printed in 1923. Williams discusses *A Hasty Bunch* in *the transatlantic review* in 1924 without notation that the book had been out for two years, and O'Brien lists it in his volume of "best stories" as coming out in 1923. The date of the volume thus cannot be definitely established. 1922 is the best guess.

McAlmon's finances. Late in 1923 the publishing went on a much sounder financial basis. At that time McAlmon received a handsome present from his father-in-law. It amounted to about fourteen thousand pounds, and with it he was enabled to publish much more widely. Until now he had simply printed a few books; at this point he undertook publishing seriously. In no time he was besieged by authors bearing manuscripts until his hotel room bulged with papers. He turned to his friend William Bird for help.

William Bird was a practicing journalist who was interested in printing. After founding the Consolidated Press Association with David Lawrence in 1919 and serving as the general manager of its Washington office, he had come to Paris as its European manager in 1920. Born in Buffalo, New York, in 1889, he was educated at Trinity College, Hartford, Connecticut, in the class of 1912. He became something of an expert on wines, and his little book on the subject has gone through several editions over the years. He had had an interest in printing since childhood, and in Paris he discovered a French journalist, Roger Dévigne, on the Ile Saint-Louis, who was printing books on an ancient hand press. Bird acquired a full series of Caslon type and hired Dévigne to print English books for him. Very shortly, in the winter of 1921-1922, an adjoining shop fell vacant, and Bird set up independently, with an ancient press of his own. It was perhaps two hundred years old. The books he printed thereafter, all done in his spare time, were produced slowly, so slowly that the ambitious Hemingway, a book of whose Bird had agreed to print, became impatient. Bird financed his publishing out of his own pocket, as a hobby; he doubts if it cost him more than golf costs many men.[22]

In the spring of 1922 Bird attended the Genoa Economic Conference as a journalist. There he met Hemingway, who was attending as a correspondent. Hemingway suggested that Bird enlist Ezra Pound's help in finding good copy, and when Bird returned to Paris, he went to see Pound. After reflecting for a couple of days, Pound suggested a series of six related books to appear over a period of a few months. Bird agreed, and in the summer of 1922 Pound became the first editor of the Three Mountains Press. In a letter to William Carlos Williams, Pound explained the terms under which the books were to be printed. Each volume was to be short, about fifty pages long, and to be issued in an edition of some three hundred fifty copies. The author was to receive fifty dollars upon acceptance of his manuscript, another fifty dollars later. Appearance in the series was not

[22] Unless otherwise indicated, the information about Bird and the Three Mountains Press comes from private correspondence.

to preclude subsequent publication. "Yeats's sister's press in Ireland," Pound wrote, referring to the celebrated Cuala Press, "has brought him a good deal in this way. I got nearly as much from my little book with them as from the big Macmillan edtn. of *Noh*."[23] Pound continues his letter to Williams with his usual gaiety, "It's hell the way I always seem to get sucked into editing something or other." The letter ends, "As Bird says, he can make money issuing bibliographies, that is NOT what he wants." The subsequent series which Pound got together included work by himself, Williams, Ford Madox Ford, Hemingway, B. C. Windeler (whose volumes of poems were subsequently published by the Oxford Press) and Miss B. M. Gould Adams.

Hemingway introduced Bird to McAlmon in 1922. When he and Bird joined forces, Bird printed a list of books headed "Contact Editions, including books printed at the Three Mountains Press." Bird planned that the Three Mountains was to be a printing office, Contact Editions was to be a publishing house. Books produced on his press were to bear the Three Mountains Press label, and the others were to be marked Contact Editions. The distinction was never maintained, however, primarily because of McAlmon's impatience with detail. McAlmon put both labels on almost everything he published. By 1924 Bird's printing office at 29, Quai D'Anjou, Ile Saint-Louis, became the headquarters of Contact Editions—Three Mountains Press. At the same address, incidentally, Bird found a tiny office for Ford Madox Ford to use when editing *the transatlantic review;* and on Thursdays, when the press did not operate, Ford used the downstairs area for his celebrated receptions.[24] As proof of his gratitude to Bird and his high esteem for both, Ford dedicated the second of the Tietjens novels, *No More Parades* (1925), to Bird and published some of McAlmon's fiction in his *review*.

Though they published some books together, McAlmon and Bird continued as independent publishers, joining forces to facilitate distribution of their books. They kept a single financial accounting, but of course they made no money. When they extended credit to American bookstores, most accounts went unpaid; and when books published in France were shipped to the United States, they were frequently held up on the docks, sometimes for long periods. Once the books reached the bookstores in New York, they were ignored by reviewers, except, perhaps, in brief notes which sneered that such-and-such a book had been printed in France by the expatriates. Generally

---

[23] Pound, *Letters*, pp. 183-184.
[24] Douglas Goldring, *The Last Pre-Raphaelite* (London, 1948), pp. 230-231.

Bird did not consult McAlmon about the books he was printing, and McAlmon did not consult Bird about his. When McAlmon showed him some of his own manuscript, Bird picked out "Miss Knight" and two other stories of Berlin night life; and the book he made of them, *Distinguished Air,* was one of the eight hand-printed Three Mountains Press books. (A bibliography of all books produced by the Contact Publishing Company and the Three Mountains Press will be found in the appendix.)

But expatriate publishing had no future. McAlmon could not get his books distributed nor accepted in the United States, their natural destination. He had come to a dead end, and his interest waned.[25] Furthermore, in 1926 Bird sold his press to Nancy Cunard, and in 1929 he moved his office and sold all the remaining volumes that were stored there to "a man named Schwartz." There were some five or six hundred of these, and they brought one hundred fifty dollars. After 1926 McAlmon and Bird no longer saw much of one another, for McAlmon did not remain long in Paris. Bird stayed on as director of the Consolidated Press Association until 1933, when it was dissolved, and then as chief foreign correspondent for the New York *Sun.* McAlmon managed to publish three books in 1929, but by this time his heart was no longer in it. Except for a brief considera- tion of Moss and Kamin's proposition in 1932, 1929 marks the end of McAlmon's career in publishing.

Though McAlmon's Contact Publishing Company was far and away the most important expatriate press in Paris, others also at- tempted to bring out interesting books. In order to fill out this ac- count of avant-garde publishing, I should at least mention the other publishers-in-exile. Sylvia Beach was the most important of them.

Miss Beach, an old resident of Paris, had a bookstore on the rue de l'Odeon, which was the hangout for English and American writers living in Paris. It had the picturesque name of Shakespeare & Co. Though she did not, apparently, aspire to general publication, unlike A. and C. Boni in New York and Pascal Covici in Chicago, when it seemed unlikely that *Ulysses* could get into print through commercial channels, she took on the task of publishing it. She saw the book off to the printer, Maurice Darantière of Dijon, and put it on sale at her shop. Later she published Joyce's volume of poems, *Pomes Penyeach* (1927) and still later *An Exagmination of James Joyce* (1929). Miss Beach, however, was unwilling and unable to undertake general publishing from her bookshop.

[25] Donald C. Gallup has published a detailed account of "The Making of *The Making of Americans,*" Gertrude Stein's "long" book which McAlmon published, in *The New Colophon, A Book Collectors' Miscellany* (New York, 1950); pp. 54-74.

Later in the decade other keepers of Paris bookshops attempted to become publishers. By 1927 Edward W. Titus, who had a bookstore in Montparnasse, was attempting it. Titus, a well-to-do lawyer and the husband of Helena Rubinstein, tried to introduce "business-like methods into the press work of the exiles."[26] He did not endear himself to them. He published such books as Mary Butts's *Imaginary Letters* (1928), Manuel Komroff's *The Voice of Fire*, Ludwig Lewisohn's *The Case of Mr. Crump; Ringaring*, a translation of Schnitzler's *Der Reigen* by Lily Wolfe and Edward W. Titus, and *Rococo*, a poem by Ralf Cheever Dunning. When Ernest Walsh died, he took over *This Quarter*, which had had three brilliant numbers. For a time assisted by Samuel Putnam, he edited it, but shortly it ceased to appear.

There were several small expatriate publishing houses not attached to bookstores, notably Pool and the Hours Press. Pool, a publishing house having its headquarters in Switzerland, appeared in 1927. This house, supported and managed by Bryher—McAlmon's former wife—and Kenneth Macpherson, her second husband, brought out a few books and an important review of films, photography and books called *Close-Up* (1927-1933). In addition to several books by Bryher—*Civilians, Film Problems of Soviet Russia* (with Kenneth Macpherson) and *The Light-Hearted Student* (with Trude Weiss)—Pool published two books by Macpherson—*Pool-reflection* and *Gaunt Island*. Bryher and Macpherson also published a novel dealing with the English public school. It was called *Why Do They Like It?* and was written by E. L. Black, with a foreword by Dorothy Richardson. It received an excellent review in *The Hound and Horn*—I,i (Sept. 1927), 64-65—and has since not been heard of. A year later, 1928, Nancy Cunard, daughter of Yeats's friend Lady Cunard, having bought the Three Mountains Press from William Bird, established the Hours Press just outside Paris. She brought out a revised edition of *Peronnik the Fool* by George Moore; a French translation of Lewis Carroll's *The Hunting of the Snark; The Probably Music of Beowulf* and *A Draft of XXX Cantos* (1930) by Ezra Pound; *One Day* by Norman Douglas and other books. All Miss Cunard's books were published in limited editions of three hundred copies.

Other than McAlmon's Contact Publishing Company, the most important expatriate press of the Twenties was Harry and Caresse Crosby's The Black Sun Press. Because it continues to operate to this day, it has had opportunity to produce a number of important books. Harry Crosby, a nephew of J. P. Morgan, a Harvard man and listed

---

[26] Parry, p. 339.

in the Social Register, "resigned from the Paris branch of the Morgan Bank in the spring of 1927 so that he and his wife might devote themselves to poetry."[27] Shortly they founded a publishing house, primarily to publish their own work. In 1928 they branched out into a somewhat different kind of publishing: fine editions of such writers as Oscar Wilde and Edgar Allan Poe; and then later in 1929 they printed D. H. Lawrence's *Sun*. Subsequently The Black Sun Press produced important works by contemporary writers, like Archibald MacLeish. Eugene Jolas, Kay Boyle, James Joyce, all in 1929; Hart Crane, Pound and MacLeish again in 1930; and in 1932, a series of distinguished reprints to which McAlmon contributed a volume.

McAlmon's Contact Publishing Company and the other expatriate presses were more like private than commercial presses. Each reflected the interests and eccentricities of its owner, irrespective of public demand or opinion. The private press has never been an important factor in American publishing, and it was not at this period. On the other hand, in England between 1915 and 1930 private presses attempted what the expatriate presses attempted in France. The most celebated of these is the Hogarth Press, started almost on a fluke by Leonard and Virginia Woolf and profitably continuing to this day. The Beaumont Press, founded the same year (1917), also had a distinguished, though hardly revolutionary, history. At this time, John Rodker attempted, with his Ovid Press, to "bring before the public work that was considered advanced." He published Pound's *Mauberly* in 1920, *Ara Vus Prec* by Eliot in 1919 and other interesting volumes; but by 1921 he was forced by lack of general public interest to turn to general publishing. In 1928 Robert Graves and Laura Riding founded the Seizin Press, but after a few titles, it too ceased to publish. Only Miss Elizabeth Corbet Yeats's Cuala Press, from 1902 onward, flourished, and it was supported by some twenty volumes of W. B. Yeats's work.[28] It is perhaps significant that the Cuala Press was never hospitable to general experimental writing. It published the figures of the "Irish Renaissance."

Since the period of McAlmon's activities, since 1929, the commercial houses have accepted the old revolutionaries: Random House publishes Gertrude Stein and William Carlos Williams, two who earlier had been neglected by commercial houses; T. S. Eliot has become one of Harcourt, Brace's very full stable of first-rate poets,

---

[27] Millicent Bell, "The Black Sun Press: 1927 to the Present," *Books at Brown*, XVII, 1-2 (Jan., 1955), p. 3. This is a complete treatment of this subject and contains a bibliography of the books the press brought out.

[28] For a general account of the activities of private presses, see Ransom, *op. cit.* This book is somewhat out of date, but it is invaluable for the period down to 1928.

and a real money-maker; James Joyce's *Ulysses* is a best-seller in the Modern Library; Hemingway remains with Scribner's. Pound is at home with New Directions. Indeed, New Directions looks after all the old revolutionaries. Oddly enough, only McAlmon has no publisher. Though these writers fare reasonably well now, for many years the writer in reaction against the established canons of literary excellence had had no help; and this McAlmon had attempted to provide. His help was only temporary, but it was considerable. "When a man like McAlmon goes down, others go with him," Dr. Williams has written. "In fact, to a greater or lesser degree, the whole front of good writing collapses. If it is not McAlmon, it is some other." He continues: "But when, often at the very moment of success, some prominent support is cut away, nothing for years may get published. Loose ends are left dangling, men are lost, promises that needed culture, needed protection and wit and courage to back them simply die. One book, here and there, gets a preliminary hearing and remains isolated, while the overwhelming flood of insensitive drivel floods the market."[29] McAlmon had seen to it that several important writers got a hearing. He helped them when they needed it most; and when he went down, it was not without loss.

[29] *Autobiography*, pp. 265-266.

McAlmon's Books

McAlmon's critical assumptions were in several respects those of his time. He and his contemporaries in the Twenties were concerned that "art" not get between them and their reactions to the world they lived in. They thought that conventional language—the language of the genteel tradition—too frequently dictated what the writer could say about experience, and it dictated often what the nature of the experience itself could be. To liberate themselves from what they thought was a dead tradition, they went into exile.

Ezra Pound had anticipated them. Rejecting the essentially verbal quality of late Victorian poetry, he and the Imagists in London had attempted to free the writer from the conventional way of looking at the world. The tenets of Imagism which Pound formulated were concerned with the immediate presentation of the "thing" uncontaminated by language. From their foreign places, where they asserted their independence of a burdensome past, the "lost generation" attempted to record immediate experience unmixed with extraneous literary associations. They strove to record only what they knew. McAlmon and Williams wrote in 1921: "We seek only contact with the local conditions which confront us. We believe that in the perfection of that contact is the beginning not only of the concept of art among us but the key to the technique also."[1] This declaration is a restatement of Pound's basic thesis.

In his own time McAlmon was admired for his determined efforts to be independent of a limiting English tradition. "Robert McAlmon is not concerned with the parade of English as the English do it," a contemporary critic wrote. "The juice, the sap, the ripeness of a person is in his writing. No obstacle of English language in the way of ornament, clever paradox, and the like is allowed to spoil its purity.

---

[1] *Contact,* 1 (Dec., 1921), p. 10.

"Is this what is wrong with English writers (in our islands), this unconvincing English?" the critic asks. "English writers still write in the English tradition and are perfectly satisfied.

"The American writer is not faced with this problem. His English is a new form and a good one too. Robert McAlmon should be read in England and France."[2]

Because he disliked verbal flourishing and what he took to be aesthetic posturing, McAlmon came increasingly to prefer "documentary, autobiographic and biographic things." His sense of the here and now was so strong, his desire for the presentation of the factual became so insistent, that at last he preferred history to fiction. This demand for authenticity led him ultimately to a rejection of the imagined. His own writing was largely autobiographical, and factual. He thought, "With a novel one must grant altogether too much to the author's sensibility, delicacy, power of insight, and capacity to create a work which is in itself a unique and distinguished organism."[3]

If McAlmon attempted in prose what the Imagists had attempted in verse—the direct presentation of experience— he differed from them by insisting that the experience which he put down be exclusively his own, what he had actually known. He wanted his writing to contain Robert McAlmon—good, bad or indifferent. It was only through the truthful detail of his individual experience that art could be created, he thought; he could write only about what he knew. In this respect he was the heir of Emerson, Thoreau and the New England preachers of self-reliance. Like them he reacted against the gathering uniformity which would wipe out individual differences. He wanted to celebrate himself, his eccentricities and his nobilities. He wanted to record the particular life he had known, unfalsified by literary attitudes. Adamantly he sought to retain his individuality and, through local detail, read universal significance.

In 1925, McAlmon's Contact Editions published a volume entitled *Contact Collection of Contemporary Writers*. In it were selections from the "works in progress" of many of the significant writers of the time. McAlmon after inviting each to contribute had apparently exercised no editorial control over what they brought to him. The table of contents reads like a roll of honor. The alphabetized contributors were: Djuna Barnes, Bryher, Mary Butts, Norman Douglas, Havelock Ellis, Ford Madox Ford, Wallace Gould, Ernest Hemingway, Marsden Hartley, H. D., John Herrmann [sic], James Joyce, Mina Loy, Robert McAlmon, Ezra Pound, Dorothy Richardson, May Sin-

---

[2] Ethel Moorhead, "Robert McAlmon's Village," *This Quarter*, I, 1 (1925), pp. 269-270. This is the only review in a very distinguished number.

[3] *Being Geniuses Together*, p. 120.

clair, Edith Sitwell, Gertrude Stein and William Carlos Williams. This volume throws into relief the literary interests of McAlmon's contemporaries and shows the relationship of his writing to contemporaneous writing.

All of the stories, poems and essays in the collection show a marked interest in psychology. Though the writers are interested in how characters react to events, they are not interested in the events themselves. The writers' concern is with the interior life. This is as true of Ford's excellent episode from *No More Parades* as it is of Joyce's episode from *Finnegan's Wake* and Hemingway's "Soldier's Home." Perhaps more important, few of these writers, with the notable exception of May Sinclair, construct a story or a poem or a piece of criticism which is entirely independent of themselves. They do not regard art as an "escape from personality," to borrow from Eliot, so much as a display of it. Reading these pieces, one can spot the figure with whom the writer identifies himself, and in most of the selections one comes fearfully close to observing a kind of narcissism. Krebs in "Soldier's Home" is not absolutely distinguishable from Hemingway; the women in the fiction by lady writers lead one inevitably back to the lady writers. Even Williams, in his praise of Marianne Moore, rather self-consciously praises himself. Each of these writers has a private axe to grind.

May Sinclair, however, constructs a ghost story which is entirely independent of herself. It is not an extension of her ego; this is a thing made, an artifact, not a bit of self-revelation. This *Contact Collection* suggests that McAlmon's generation thought of art as a kind of romantic exhibitionism. It is as though each of these writers had said, "Let me tell you about myself." When the writer is perceptive, like Ford and Norman Douglas, the result is interesting; but in lesser hands it is silly if not worse.

McAlmon's piece is much like the others, but it offends by its confessional quality. In his haste to give an immediate impression of his experience, he has not revised what seem almost to be pages from his diary. The story is not organized, except chronologically, the conversations do not build to climaxes, and the characters are indicated but not developed. The attitude of the writer toward his material is adolescent. In fact, the story insults the reader by assuming that it is interesting of itself, by the mere fact of its existence. It is not *made*. Fortunately McAlmon published a good number of pieces that are superior to this one, but this "extract" shows his habitual direction, just as this volume shows a common attitude of the period. These writers all seem more interested in themselves than in the world they live in.

McAlmon draws extensively on his own personal experience for his fiction; and at best his sketches, anecdotes and reminiscenses have the flow of life in them. He distrusts plot generally, thinking that formal arrangement of incident falsifies experience which is not formal; and he distrusts logical organization for the same reason. As we read we move from one personal detail, one private incident, to the next with the freedom from purpose we experience outside fiction. As a result, the stories never contain dramatic suspense. They have only the suspense that we feel in life: what will happen next? as distinguished from, what does this detail mean in this place? The stories have abundant material for plotting; something is always happening and people are always in conflict. But the conflicts are undeveloped and pass without comment. McAlmon does not interpret. He records. The pleasures to be taken from his work are the pleasures that one may take in the factual. For McAlmon, a piece of writing must be faithful to observable experience; and judged by this standard, his has considerable merit. He never "made Midwestern speech into a prose, living and alert," like Hemingway.[4] But his fiction contains verifiable truth. He gives an account of a Midwestern meat-and-potato world where nightingales and goddesses have no place. His great virtue is candor.

THE VOLUMES

McAlmon's first book was a volume of verse and prose meditations entitled *Explorations*. It was published by The Egoist Press whose guiding spirit was Harriet Weaver. Harriet Weaver, Joyce's angel, had published Eliot's *Prufrock and Other Observations* in 1917. Now in 1921 she saw that McAlmon's book was published. Her endorsement of it is a high commendation.

The slim volume (eighty pages) contained sixteen poems under the general heading, "Surf of the Dead Sea"; seven poems, subtitled "Air Rhythms," which had appeared in part in *Poetry;* thirty-three prose meditations called "Mood Decisions"; fourteen somewhat longer prose selections called "Prose Sketches"; and seventeen pieces called "From Adolescence to Intelligence." McAlmon says of the volume in his autobiography, "At this time the Egoist Press published a book of my poetry, *Explorations,* but as nobody paid it any attention I need not apologize, and can dare to say that much worse had been done before and is being done yet by others."[5] It was reviewed in *Poetry*

---

[4] John Peale Bishop, "Homage to Hemingway," in *After the Genteel Tradition,* Malcolm Cowley, ed., (New York, 1937), p. 195.
[5] *Being Geniuses Together,* p. 9.

by his friend, Emanuel Carnevali. "McAlmon seeks—it is hard to say just what he seeks; there is a spirit of quest in this book," Carnevali wrote. "The tedium and nausea of sophistication, with the struggle thereof, are emphasized in this slim book. Yet McAlmon is sometimes simple and direct."[6]

The volume, obviously by a very young man, contains poems about the difficulties of the writing, about the suffering creator and about sex. A great number of them are about frustrations of one kind or another, some almost like dream-fantasies. McAlmon's artistic purposes are clear, however. Here are some typical lines, from "Form Destructionist—Sculptor":

Three times he had destroyed beginnings of his last work,
Fearing that they were not authentic expressions
Of impulses indigenous of his own contacts.
Given the alien substance of some trifling annoyance,
His nature could furnish nacre
For finer pearls of concept and execution than these.

Few readers would find the verse in this volume remarkable. The rhythms are not especially attractive; the metaphors are not sharp nor fresh. The poems are illuminating to one concerned with their author's developing critical attitudes but probably to nobody else. Indeed in them one can detect a certain artiness, a certain posturing, which is not altogether agreeable. The prose passages in the volume are even less satisfactory, for they contain the same faults of prosiness and posturing which is never altogether absent from the poems. One can not be surprised that the volume caused no stir.

The first book McAlmon printed himself, inaugurating the Contact Publishing Company, was his own *A Hasty Bunch*. Like all his books, it was brought out in a small edition, some three hundred copies, and is now rare. It can be obtained only in a few libraries which specialize in rare books of the Twentieth Century, and very occasionally through dealers. Since all McAlmon's books are practically unobtainable and yet deserve a place in a record of the literature of the Twenties, a reasonably full account of them seems called for here.

A Hasty Bunch was written, McAlmon tells us, in six weeks, probably in 1921. He writes of it: "In the daytime I was busy writing the short stories which went into *A Hasty Bunch*, a title which Joyce suggested because he found my American use of language racy. I

---

[6] *Poetry*, XX (June, 1922), p. 157.

was at that six weeks. . . ."⁷ It contains twenty-three sketches, nine "Momentary Essays" and "A Protoplasmic Farce" called "Creation." Several of the stories deal with characters and situations more fully exploited later in *Village* (1925). In the nine "Momentary Essays" McAlmon attempts to put down his immediate responses to objects and situations. Like pencil sketches, they have the charm of quick perceptions.

A Hasty Bunch was not widely distributed. Unlike some other Contact books, it did not appear in New York "republished" by a bookstore, nor was it offered for sale in the United States until Moss and Kamin advertised it in 1932. In effect it was printed privately. O'Brien listed the volume in his "Best Books of Short Stories of 1924," and he singled out the story "Elsie" for special distinction by listing it on his "Roll of Honor." William Carlos Williams discussed the volume at some length in an essay he contributed to *the transatlantic review* entitled "Robert McAlmon's Prose." He wrote of it: "In his total discarding of every literary support, along with other things goes finally 'le mot juste.' Villon could not exist now if there were the faintest feeling about his writing that he had sought to be effective. McAlmon has seen this instantly. 'Le mot juste' is the ready word, it has no other significance. This is fundamental. There cannot be in literature a seeking for words. Round this finally the whole feeling of life in McAlmon's composition grows. It is dangerous ground, but good writing is rare."⁸ Williams chooses "A Vacation's Job" and the "Momentary Essays" for special praise. Ford Madox Ford, an editor of distinguished ability, selected "Elsie" from this volume to include in the first issue of his new *transatlantic review*.

In one of the stories, "The Futility of Energy," McAlmon says clearly what he is attempting in his fiction: "Rightly or wrongly, Raymond believed that art must be reflective, discerning; must create new experience, explore, and re-interpret in a manner that withstands the sternest intellectual diagnosis, but with a re-interpretation that is simply more discerning recordation rather than a preachment. Form against form, colour against colour, to make a formal and colour music with more than decorative impact, and back of these a mature

⁷ *Being Geniuses Together*, p. 21. Several of the pieces in *A Hasty Bunch* were reprinted: "Elsie," in *the transatlantic review*, I, i (1924), pp. 59-64: "A Vacation's Job," in *transition*, 5 (1927), pp. 66-73, (a version inferior to the one in the volume); "Obsequies for the Dead" (retitled "The Laughing Funeral"), "Temperament" and "New York Harbour," in *The Indefinite Huntress and Other Stories* (Paris, 1932). "New York Harbour" was also reprinted in *The Morada*, 5 (1930), pp. 8-12. "Sing the Baby to Sleep, Marietta" was later translated into French and published in *la revue europeenne* (1 Jan., 1928).

⁸ I, 3 (1924), p. 362.

realization of life's signification, was what he sought to express. To have accepted reality, mortality, pain, obscenity, tedium—to the extent of being a little incapable of knowing which is which in the routine chaos of experience—and still to believe in exploration. . . ." (p. 257).

At best McAlmon succeeds in communicating a fresh response to newly observed experience. He succeeds in recording reactions unspoiled by second-hand associations. As a result much of his work reads as though it were written by a man only this morning born into the world, a man seeing all the earth for the first time. In so far as he succeeds in capturing this freshness, his stories are pleasing. They are often faulty, however, for simple technical reasons. "Obsequies of the Dead," for example, does not succeed entirely, because its point of view is inconsistent with our experience. Benny, a young boy, goes to the funeral of his friend, the village cynic, where he hears him eulogized. The incongruity of the pietistic eulogy and the old man's iconoclasm forces Benny into spasms of laughter. He runs from the funeral chapel to sit on its steps where he is joined, soon, by other laughing villagers. Laughing and indignant simultaneously, they blame him for disrupting the ceremony.

McAlmon has material for a funny and significant story here, but it does not succeed because Benny is too aware of his own emotions. Benny is made to understand too fully why he reacts as he does. If he had been allowed to react only, if the interpretation and analysis had been supplied by an older, a more experienced Benny looking back, reporting the incident, the story would be more consistent with our knowledge of boys. McAlmon has observed the fakery surrounding funerals honestly. His failure is in the writing, in the construction of the story after the initial inspiration. He wastes his material in his haste.

"A Vacation's Job" and "Summer," both long stories, are the best in this volume. They keep a consistent point of view, that of a footloose young man in search of—what? Is he looking for a cause that will require his loyalty, a task that will engulf his enthusiasm? These plotless stories record the young man's drifting, and these wanderings form a kind of purposeless pattern. "A Vacation's Job" begins in David's mother's kitchen where David (McAlmon, clearly) receives a telegraphic offer of a job on a levee. He goes to his college campus where he says goodbye to the girls, badgers his teachers into giving him credits he hasn't earned, catches a train for the valley. He finds when he arrives that he and the friend who had got him the job are no longer congenial, but he also finds that Harry Gallego, an illiterate Mexican with impractical aspirations, is a fine companion.

On one Saturday night he goes to a dance held by the Mexicans; on another occasion he goes to a celebration held by the local Negroes. He recognizes in the Negroes and the Mexicans, a bit enviously, a resignation which he does not possess. He feels himself consciously set apart from them, for they seem able to live fully, they do not sacrifice one part of their nature to another. In time a flood comes, washing away the levee on which he and the other men have worked for weeks; this flood scene is one of the most impressive in the story. And at last David drives back to Los Angeles with Old Man Woods, across the desert at night, arriving in his mother's kitchen. "You can't drift forever," his mother says. "You might just as well settle here." And David replies ironically, "I might just as well not, too. . . . You just leave my generation's problems to be solved by the members of that generation" (p. 215).

The story ends here, where it began, with nothing settled. Its theme is the theme of all McAlmon's fiction. He attempts to record the restless drift of a generation without roots, which does not feel itself responsible for the world into which it is born, which questions all the values that the preceding generations have established. The second story, "Summer," is similar to this one. In it the young man, this time frankly "I," goes to work in the Dakota harvest fields and moves on, in time, to Montana, only to return to his mother's home, at last, and a breakfast of oatmeal.

These stories have the great virtues of vigor and novelty. They do not oversimplify character or choice, and they give an unbiased picture of the world in which the action takes place. Perhaps their principal value is their fidelity to place and time. Certainly their principal shortcoming is stylistic. The constant variations of "said" are annoying; and the sentences in the dialogue are much too drawn out and involved. The diction is generally impure. The adverbs, for example, seem constructed on the spot, by the arbitrary addition of -ly to any convenient word.

These stylistic faults are due to haste; they are the results of excessive impatience with detail. McAlmon never slicked up his stories. Perhaps the very roughness is part of the tone which McAlmon strives for: raw spontaneity. But this rawness, alas, is self-defeating. A half-told anecdote does not seem more "immediate" than one fully developed. Rather, it leaves the reader uncomfortable, for in it good material remains unrealized. One could wish that McAlmon had polished up his manuscripts before printing them.

The second collection of McAlmon's short stories was called *A Companion Volume*. Like the earlier collection, it is not dated, but this one is marked: "Published by Contact Publishing Co." It was undoubtedly brought out in 1923. *A Companion Volume* contains eleven stories of varying length and kind. O'Brien names it along with the earlier volume in his list of best books of short stories published between October, 1923 and October, 1924. He singles out the story "Three Generations of the Same" for special commendation.

Though the stories lack developed conflict, the quality of the fiction in this volume is much higher than that of the previous collection. Williams, in a critical essay published in *the transatlantic review*. notes the improvement: "Several of these stories are immeasurably superior to anything in *A Hasty Bunch*. An occasional patchiness of the earlier work due to insufficient organization of the story as a whole, and a too headlong attempt at characterization—has in the best of the present work entirely disappeared."[9] He singles out three stories for praise: "Three Generations of the Same," "Spectators" and "An Illiterate but Interesting Woman." The last of these was later, in 1929, reprinted in *The New American Caravan*.[10] "For me," Williams writes, "McAlmon is satisfying and diverting because of that in his work which is bare statement of a certain sort of fact."

Like the earlier volume, this one contains some stories of autobiographical wandering. One, "A North Dakota Surveying Party," is like "Summer" and "A Vacation's Job." It is less satisfactory than they because of its offensive diction and self-conscious straining after effect. The beginning paragraph will illustrate. The story begins: "He stood looking at the grassy prairie stretched rollingly horizonward on all sides of him, and standing, disquieted within himself, attempted to think, dimly revolting against all that reflection put within his consciousness. Was the horizon farther away, or nearer to him, because of the endlessness of space, which expanded for his senses into an all enveloping clarity of sunlight and breeze, and then, on the ebb of a thought, shriveled into an imprisoning nothingness through which all his emotions and mind could rage cagedly, and without attainment" (p. 37). The coined adverbs—cagedly, rollingly—irritate and snag the eye, and the abstract nouns—consciousness, endlessness, nothingness, attainment—work against the sense of immediate physical experience that McAlmon is striving for.

The other long story of the Midwest, "Putting a Town on the Map," suffers less from this kind of diction. In it a couple of young men, wanting to make some money, persuade the merchants of a small town to support an advertising campaign that will push their

---

[9] "Robert McAlmon's Prose, I. A Companion Volume," 2 (1924), p. 215.
[10] Alfred Kreymborg, Lewis Mumford, Paul Rosenfeld, eds., (New York, 1929), pp. 161-164.

community as a resort area. The young men take a cut from the advertising they sell. If in the selling they are forced to play both ends against the middle, they do not hestitate. Though the story deals with the kind of situation Sinclair Lewis might have developed, it is totally unlike *Main Street* and *Babbitt*. It is not at all satirical. If McAlmon's story is not sleek and finished like Lewis's it is honest. The people whom the boys meet are not caricatures, and the boys themselves are not oversimplied schemers. Neither the people nor the town is deliberately distorted. There is a candor in the handling of the details that is quite unlike Lewis's professional exaggerations. McAlmon keeps his eye on the object that he is discussing. He is not concerned with the effect his detail may have on a reader.

The best story in the collection is "Evening on the Riviera." It was reprinted in McAlmon's later collection, *The Indefinite Huntress and Other Stories* (1932). Tootles, a rich sixty-year-old widow, finds herself on the Riviera surrounded by lazy young men who are looking for a free ride. The story recounts the activities of one evening: the arrival of a pair of gigolos and other hangers-on, the attempted gaiety, the casual abandon of the easily bored. Desperately attempting to escape ennui, everyone drinks immoderately. The story is tough, straightforward and unpretty; and it is also funny. Tootles is pathetic, funny, ridiculous and disgusting, all at once.

The story can bear comparison to Scott Fitzgerald's stories of the Riviera. Unlike his stories, there are no glamourous movie stars in "Evening on the Riviera," and here no heroic young doctors give up their fabulous talents for demanding and fabulous wives. McAlmon's cars, like Fitzgerald's, are driven at top speed, but McAlmon's cars are not all Rolls Royces. "An Evening on the Riviera" has the great virtue of truth, for its author does not take Hollywood's view of anything. The characters here are not self-conscious: they may be desperate, but they are not poseurs; they are not waiting for a scenario and a director. If Fitzgerald treats his characters with a deathly seriousness, McAlmon treats his dispassionately. Fitzgerald's account of the lost generation is ultimately adolescent; McAlmon's account may be rough, but it is adult.

The persons in all the stories in this volume are without purpose. The stories meander plotlessly; their lack of direction is proper to their subjects. In "Three Generations of the Same," one character says: "But it's the wondering what to do with myself that gets me" (p. 154); in "The Moving Picture Crew," somebody says: "I don't care about anything; don't believe in anything. I just drag myself around because I happen to have life though I don't find anything in it I want now" (p. 191). And Jimmy, a young man in the story "Aunt

Mary," thinks about his old relatives: "They are, that life may go on; that crows shall fly and cows shall be fed; that houses are kept for Uncle Johns who employ farmhands that plant and harvest grains; for grains to be the staff of life. But why?" (p. 228). These puzzled people are not satirized, though we may occasionally smile at them; and McAlmon brings no moral judgment against their aimless lives. He accepts what he sees, and he does not "glamourize" it. As usual he does not slant his material. Nobody would want to imitate the lives of these lost souls, but McAlmon does not ask us to be contemptuous of them either.

Reading these stories, we approach a real imaginative world, not a papier-mâché mock-up built for an occasion or for a plot. We can not live in this world, as we live in the created worlds of Faulkner and Hemingway and the early Dos Passos; but in these stories we catch a glimpse of a reality. We become impatient that McAlmon did not work over his first drafts, that he did not rewrite, clarifying his inspiration. If he had, his books could take their place with the best of his generation. As it is, he does not have the faults of professionalism, and he has the virtue of integrity. One's persistent disappointment that these stories are not better is in itself a kind of praise. Unfortunately McAlmon was too impatient to learn his craft.

The next volume of McAlmon's work to appear was *Post-Adolescence*. Although its date of publication is not given (it was 1923), the volume is marked "Published by Contact Publishing Co." and contains the notice, "Written previously to A Hasty Bunch in 1920." Though this book masquerades as a novella, its central figure, Peter, is so clearly the author that it reads like slightly dramatized autobiography. It has the virtues of a first-rate memoir: intimacy and candor; and we come from it with a thorough understanding of its central character. William Carlos Williams in his discussion of it calls it "a *journal intime*" and says: "On the surface the book sets out to depict many sorts of people encountered among the city streets. But the final impression, and the fact, is that here is only one person, a young man hounded in his own body by the realities of love and sex, which just at the close of adolescence are seen introspectively possessing him. These appearances come to him in the persons of his friends."[11]

Peter in *Post-Adolescence,* like the Bennys and Davids of the other stories, searches for explanation and purpose, but he searches with positive ebullience. This was McAlmon's first book—though it was not printed first—and its youth is obvious and delightful. Here are

[11] "Robert McAlmon's Prose, II. Post-Adolescence," *the transatlantic review*, II, 2 (1924), pp. 216-217.

its concluding paragraphs: "As the wind went by him, coldly stinging, he could sense that it was dancing with him, but he could not leap up and dance, whirling around, jumping, striking the wind, here in the city streets.

"But he'd walk miles, walk off this spurt of energy. To the devil with any kind of care. Life would happen as it would happen, and he would not allow it to batter him into a gray mass of lethargic protoplasm; not so long as energy enough remained within him to offer an exhilarated response to life. There was nothing to know but wonder, generally, and tiny finite facts that banged him in the face, and the rest could stay open, and unsolved" (p. 119).

There is no more plot in this novel than in the stories. Peter wanders about Greenwich Village, seeing his friends, drinking, dancing, talking. The incidents are recounted chronologically, without apparent thematic arrangement, and the result is pleasing, natural and unaffected. The irritating mannerisms are here at a minimum. There are fewer vulgar variations of the word "said," fewer coined adjectives, shorter speeches which seem truer to real voices; the various scenes, though casually related to one another, have an organization and a shape. And on every page there is the gaiety of a young man enjoying his adventurous life.

Post-Adolescence deserves considerably more attention than it has ever received, for a number of reasons. First, it gives a frank and unsentimental picture of a young man in "post-adolescence." E. M. Forster has remarked that ninety percent of novels is taken up with love—I am paraphrasing— but that love occupies at most only ten percent of our extrafictional experience. Love, he notes, is almost a convention of the novel.[12] The proportion is righted here. Sex plays a large part in the book, as Williams points out, but the conventional love problems are ignored. This is not a conventional book: it is free of literary forms and traditional situations. It is a delightful short novel.

The book has considerable historical value, perhaps as much value as history as it has as fiction. Here is a precise account of the daily life in Bohemia, uncolored by prejudice and unforced by thesis. Unheightened, the life is reported dispassionately and in detail. McAlmon's habit of hard-boiled unsentimentalism makes him an excellent reporter on this excellent beat. Because it is so detailed, this book can be a valuable supplement to such scholarly accounts of Bohemia as Albert Parry's *Garrets and Pretenders* (New York, 1933)

[12] Chapter XI, "People," *Aspects of the Novel* (New York, 1927). See especially pp. 85-86.

and Caroline F. Ware's *Greenwich Village, 1920-1930* (Boston, 1935). It can supplement Greenwich Village memoirs, like Alfred Kreymborg's *Troubadour* (New York, 1925). McAlmon takes us to a party given by an inmate of the Village, Lola Ridge, perhaps. We learn how riotous the Villagers actually were. We observe the easy camaraderie of the impoverished and hopeful young, and the essential cheerfulness of these talented people who are out to correct the world. We see them in cafeterias, and we hear them talk. Here is *La Bohème* without fakery. Though McAlmon does not dress up the sordid details, from his book we catch a hint of the fascination of Bohemia.

The book has yet another value. It contains portraits of persons who subsequently became famous and influential. Though they bear pseudonyms, their disguises are thin. Williams appears as Jim Boyle, a young doctor who lives in New Jersey and talks about his soul; Marsden Hartley, the poet-painter, appears as Brander Ogden—this portrait is especially illuminating; Edna St. Vincent Millay appears very briefly as Vere St. Vitus; and Marianne Moore appears as Martha Wullus, complete with her mother and a job in the library. The knowing will find others in these pages. One could wish that McAlmon had revised more carefully; but as the book stands, it is an important picture of a peculiar intellectual-social milieu and its people. More important, it is a gay book by a charming young man. It does not deserve its complete oblivion.

Village: As It Happened through a Fifteen Year Period is the first of McAlmon's volumes which is dated. It appeared in 1924 "Published by Contact Publishing Co." Of all McAlmon's books this novel has been most frequently referred to, but even this one has not often been spoken of. Ima Honaker Herron considers it in her survey of *The Small Town in American Literature* (Durham, North Carolina, 1939), saying of it: "Here is a small town order which is the very antithesis of that glorified by the school of sweetness and light. In Wentworth there is no sign of the happy average of the 1900's" (pp. 407-8). And Hoffman mentions it briefly in his survey of the Twenties, calling it a "succession of illustrations of the monotony of village life, with its refrain of pointless violence."[13] Its most extended treatment is in Régis Michaud's *The American Novel To-day* (1931). "McAlmon is less optimistic than Mark Twain," he writes. "His Tom Sawyers are cynics, with their own good reasons. They are stifled by their surroundings, they are walled up alive."[14] When Ethel Moorhead re-

[13] Frederick J. Hoffman, *The Twenties*, p. 329.
[14] (Boston, 1931), pp. 262-269. Michaud's facts about McAlmon (p. 262) are inaccurate. My quotation comes from p. 264.

viewed the book in the quarterly, *This Quarter,* she used it as a club with which to beat the conservatives of a literary-British tradition. "It is not the old novel form of thrashing out to weariness the problems of impossible people," she wrote.[15] Another "literary liberal," Ford Madox Ford, printed one episode from the novel in his *transatlantic review.*[16]

Village, like McAlmon's shorter fiction, contains a good many irritating mannerisms. Probably written during McAlmon's wanderings about the continent in 1921-1923 before he undertook publishing, it was printed without thorough revision. Many pages are amateurish, for they lack unity and emphasis. The book has no central conflict and no plot, and it seems to have no organization. Like the life in the village it describes, one thing leads to another, without direction and without necessary end. The same awareness of purposelessness which is dramatized in *A Companion Volume* is here given more extended treatment. We follow the fortunes of several families, the Coltons, Hardcutts, LaBrecs, Downings, first observing the members of one family, then another. McAlmon tells us how Mrs. Hammer, who has a vague desire to "be somebody," stages a WCTU elocution contest. We learn how the girls from the Normal School duck out of their dormitories for midnight (and harmless) escapades with the local boys. We see the young people encamped on Lake Barrow for a week's outing at the Chautauqua. We watch the daily activities of the town.

Though we come away from *Village* with a composite picture of life in Wentworth, we have no sharp single impression of any of its people: they merge into a general montage. No character dominates, for our attention is directed first to one, then to another. The scenes, too, merge into a single generalized final impression. Though the various episodes occur over a fifteen year period and though we watch the young Reeves and Freemans and Scotts grow up, neither the people nor the town changes significantly. Wentworth is not different at the end of the fifteen year period from what it was at the beginning. Some of the families have risen on the social ladder, it is true, and others have declined; but the fluctuation has no pattern.

Village is held together by McAlmon's single insistent opinion: life in the Middle Western town before the war was oppressive. Generous actions of affection and kindness were suspected there of coming from sordid motives; and no two people, in this book, succeeded in establishing a sensitive relationship, not even a man and

[15] I, i (1925), p. 267. I have quoted from this review above.
[16] II, 6 (1924), pp. 655-661.

his wife. In *Village,* one character, a man, says to another, a sixteen-year-old girl:

"Can't we ever have just an affectionate impulse without people thinking it's got some bad meaning. I'd like to put my arms about you, protect you, just from growing up and knowing what you'll have to know about."

And she answers, "We had better go into the hotel now. You'll make me feel sad if we stay out here. Don't I see what becomes of people—my older brothers and sisters—O, I wish I could go away somewhere right now" (p. 222).

But the people of Wentworth can not go away. Though Don Reeves, the speaker, has been working in Minneapolis for two years, he cannot escape repression and suspicion. One young woman, having recognized in Europe possibilities that she had not suspected at home, returns only to decline apathetically. Teachers come to Wentworth driven by economic necessity; and when they leave, they find no fulfillment elsewhere. McAlmon is attacking not only the provincialism of the small Midwestern town in this book; he reacts against Puritan respectability wherever he sees it. This false respectability refuses to allow anyone, not simply the plainsman, to take delight in life for itself. It denies the body and the mind alike their pleasures. It gives the imagination no place to operate, McAlmon thinks; and it will not allow the emotions any fullness. It is pinched, narrow, negative and restrictive, and it encourages all that is shallow, hypocritical and cheap. It kills inspiration, by shutting up the interior life; and it turns sensitive young men into wanderers. "If the bloody war hadn't come on I'd have struck for Europe to see if living over there wasn't more gracious; aber mein Gott," young Peter Reynalds tells one of his friends. "It's this being an American; neither a savage, nor a civilized man. A roughneck who's a little too refined. But the devil. . ." And the friend, from whom he is isolated, tells him, "You just make problems for yourself, that's all, Pete. I don't know what you're driving at half the time" (p. 228).

Village is a much more somber book than *Post-Adolescence* or, for that matter, the volumes of short stories. It lacks their *joie de vivre,* and though it contains wry irony, it has little humor. It is filled with a kind of general disillusion, and in this it differs from McAlmon's previous fiction. We are convinced from the stories in McAlmon's two collections that life in the small town is niggardly; in *Village* we see, after a moment's consideration, that life outside it is nearly as bad. Wentworth does not have a corner on narrow, shut-in lives. Under this code of respectability, wherever it may be, a complete life is impossible. McAlmon implicitly indicts the whole ideal of American propriety. Since he records what he has seen and what he has known without comment, we come to our conclusions without prodding, and the sympathetic reader leaves *Village* knowing what life among the "respectable" must have been like. It must not have been pleasant.

In 1925 William Bird published at the Three Mountains Press a little book by McAlmon entitled *Distinguished Air (Grim Fairy Tales)*. A handsome volume with a half-leather binding and printed on fine paper, it was issued in only one hundred fifteen copies. It has become rare. The three stories it contains all deal with night life in post-war Berlin. The first, the story which gives the volume its name, was McAlmon's favorite; it is concerned with promiscuous male homosexuality. The second, "Miss Knight," also dealing with male homosexuality, is a study of a man who seems to possess only female instincts. The third story, "The Lodging House," deals with the joyless vagaries of heterosexual relationships, all of them heightened by cocaine and whiskey.

McAlmon pictures here a world of total abandon where nothing stable remains, not even sex. He records without judgment what he has observed, and the result oddly enough is not without a kind of humor, even, perhaps, a kind of gaiety. Some time later McAlmon said of the books, " . . . various French people thought the story *Miss Knight* sharp and stark presentation of a type new to literature but not to life. At any rate the stories did deal with variant types with a complete objectivity, not intent on their 'souls' and not distressed by their 'morals.' "[17] "Miss Knight" attracted much the most attention of the stories in the volume; and, on James Joyce's suggestion, it was translated into French and appeared in the French-Italian quarterly *900*. Ezra Pound also thought "Miss Knight" one of McAlmon's best.

Distinguished Air was discussed at some length by Ernest Walsh in *This Quarter* shortly after its appearance. His remarks follow the famous review of Hemingway's *In Our Time* (New York edition) in which he calls Hemingway "the shyest and proudest and sweetest smelling story-teller of my reading." Walsh says of *Distinguished Air*: "It is about Lesbians male and female if you will. He calls them *fairies*. They ought to be disgusting to the average reader but they remain comic. Just as in life they are comic. McAlmon never writes disgusting books. He isn't disgusting himself. He doesn't exclude anything from his world and is like Walt Whitman in his completeness but differs from Whitman in that he doesn't argue with his readers. He doesn't explain either. He doesn't apologize. He is a great white father watching the brood and because some of the brood are a queer

---

[17] *Being Geniuses Together*, p. 148.

lot according to the world McAlmon doesn't shut the door and refuse them what he didn't give them, their life. *Distinguished Air* is interesting as an example of what a really distinguished mind can do with difficult material. . . . McAlmon has seen the humanity that is in the lives of these twisted characters and given us the humanity and left the rest out."[18]

Here more than in any of his fiction one can see with great clarity McAlmon's essentially compassionate nature. If he is lost, wandering, a kind of cynic, deserted by the standards of his father's generation, he at least has the virtue of his shortcomings. If he can find no law which requires his allegiance, he can find no life that deserves his scorn. He does not condemn; he presents. Even when he is himself an actor in his stories, he is completely detached. Because of his objectivity, his emotions never get between the reader and the material. This objectivity, as Walsh says, turns these stories into art.

"Distinguished Air," the first story, is an account of an evening spent by the narrator and Rudge Kepler, a cartoonist, in the night clubs of post-war Berlin. We meet Foster Graham, a flip and chichi homosexual who is "unable to be direct for over a moment." Another homosexual, who is somewhat more stable, says of him: "And with this after-war atmosphere, and poverty amongst the few really likeable Germans one knows. It's all too tragic, I suppose, but I just can't feel any further about that sort of thing. People will starve to death; people will die; or kill themselves, or drink themselves to death. Now Foster has, or had, an air—real distinction—but life has become just too much for him" (p. 15). Life has become just too much for the people we meet in all three of these stories: the male whores who are close to starvation, the silly fairies who desperately pretend affections they do not feel; the degenerate aristocrats who beg marks to buy "snow"—cocaine; the college boys after a cheap thrill; the Americans who live impoverished lives in their dreadful cafes because of their psychological aberrations; the artists who cannot paint, the writers who cannot write, all the weakly talented, lost and abandoned men and women of a decaying world.

The characters come out sharp and clear in these stories, but the real subject of the book, a world askew, is even clearer. Beside them Christopher Isherwood's accounts of Berlin look soft, contrived and even sentimental; and Djuna Barnes's much praised *Nightwood*, for all its elegant prose, seems diseased. McAlmon from his cool distance does not ask us for sympathy. As a result his book is an unembarrassed account of an area of experience not frequently treated at all and

[18] *This Quarter*, I, 2 (1925-1926), p. 332.

seldom discussed without a smirk or bravado. McAlmon's documentary style for once completely succeeds. *Distinguished Air* is McAlmon's best book, for it has authenticity and detachment. It ought to earn him permanent admiration, and it certainly deserves to be republished.

After the publication of *Contact Collection of Contemporary Writers* (1925) which contained a piece of his fiction, McAlmon's next book was *The Portrait of a Generation, Including The Revolving Mirror* (1926). It consists of two general parts: a long poem of some 900 lines, "The Revolving Mirror," in which he attempts to give an account of his time; and a collection of shorter lyrics, collected under three headings, "Fragments and Miscellany," "Jewels, Vegetables, and Flesh" and "Contemporary Irritations and Didactics." The volume was published in only two hundred copies by Contact Editions, Three Mountains Press. It was reviewed in *Poetry* by Bryher, McAlmon's wife, who discussed the single long poem. It embodies, she said, the ideas of its generation. "The war, by making security a thing of disbelief, altered all values. Most people would prefer a moral order in which they could believe," she writes, and concludes, "For *Revolving Mirror* is not merely a portrait of a modern generation; it is also the biography of two continents."[19] The next spring, Ethel Moorhead said of the book, "In *The Portrait of a Generation* by Robert McAlmon we mostly lose Robert McAlmon. In this book of verse he is mostly the clever cynical observer. This is clearly all he wanted to put in. . . . His experiment is not without conceit, but it lacks self-assurance and self-confidence. For it is daring about others but not sufficiently courageous about Robert McAlmon, who in this book adopts a conscientiously intellectual tone; in which the highest moments have a fleeting and shame-faced tenderness."[20] Ernest Walsh, Miss Moorhead's co-editor of *This Quarter,* had disparaged McAlmon's poetry in a preceding issue. Régis Michaud took brief notice of the volume in his book on the American novel. McAlmon "has made himself the spokesman of the pathetic nihilism in which young Americans are struggling today. 'The Portrait of a Generation' is a handbook of pessimism mitigated with humor and fantasy."[21] Curiously, the passage from "The Revolving Mirror" that M. Michaud quotes to illustrate this pessimism is printed like prose (inaccurately). "The Revolving Mirror" was reproduced entirely in *larus* (1928), a quarterly published briefly in Lynn, Massachusetts, edited by John Sherry Mangan in America and Virgil Thomson in France.[22]

[19] XXVIII (1926), pp. 280-282.
[20] *This Quarter,* I, ii (1927), pp. 279-282; I quote from p. 281.
[21] *The American Novel Today,* p. 269.
[22] I, 5,6,7 (April-May-June, 1928) [one issue], pp. 10-39.

"The Revolving Mirror," like *The Waste Land,* is a poem of voices. Voices come to the reader from all directions and out of all history. Since McAlmon's poem did not have the benefit of Ezra Pound's severe editing, all its transitions are present. We never have to make conjectures concerning the identity of any speaker. Each section is labelled. A speaker identified as "Neurotic Correspondent" unites the various fragments. Some eleven of these fragments are labelled "Romances." Sir John Ellerman, McAlmon's father-in-law, appears in "Romance VI," Lady Ellerman in "Romance VIII," and a number of McAlmon's bistro friends are in other sections of the poem. Here is "Romance V"—the "he" is James Joyce:

> That he had been and continued to be praised
> pleased his vanity at moments
> but when drunk,
>> a drunk distinguished foreigner
>> distinguishably drunken
>>> drinking
> he wept.
>> That his father,
>> and his father's father
>> and fathers before them
>> were parents of families
>> twelve to seventeen in number,
>> But his economic circumstances—
> Neverthless:
>> "I'm a young man yet,
>> and my wife is strong.
>> I'll make me a few more
>> before it's ended by the grace of God."

Each "Romance" is a character sketch; some are dramatic monologues. Other fragments are entitled "Emphatic Decision." Here is one, a sketch of an American tourist passing judgment on what he does not understand:

> "There's Mussolini. He could do it,
> not in OUR country.
> Hand across the chest. Five minutes posturing
> with hypnotizing gaze at the audience. . . .
> Why in OUR country we'd throw eggs at him
> the second minute of his paralyzing look.
> We know all about travelling hypnotists!!"

Occasionally there is a "Historic Reminiscence." A contemporary voice narrates some historic fact and indicates a contemporary attitude toward the past. We overhear this fragment, for example:

> Of course Mary had French in her
> and she was gay. She needed it in those days.
> Darnley, you know, was a homosexual.
> Yes. . . . . . O didn't you know?
> Page boys and all that sort of thing. . . .

By the use of little bits and snatches overhead as it were, McAlmon obtains a kind of movement through historical time as well as through various contemporary societies and areas of experience. Altogether he presents a series of random snapshots of civilization. Not all of the parts are of the same excellence, but at their best they capture in a few words the spirit of a character or a situation or a type.

The poem is in free verse and attempts, sometimes successfully, to echo real speech. The verse rarely becomes more than rhythmic prose, however, and is saved from flat failure primarily by its humor and its topicality. One cannot escape the conviction that "Revolving Mirror" is a kind of response to Eliot, often almost a parody of his verse. There is no nostalgic yearning for a glorious past here, no long-ing for a Golden Age now lost. McAlmon accepts what is, without sugar coating or regrets. He is convinced that *plus ça change, plus c'est la même chose,* and he strikes out at Eliot in passing.

The poem is sardonic; and in its hardboiled way, it has a kind of cleansing asperity. Though much of it is pedestrian, to say the least, occasionally one comes across soft and romantic lines like:

> May the amber moon, enchanted,
> find high towers to meditate upon.
> Like incessant rain,
> as a phantom pain. . . . . .
> Steel-brittle Aphrodite of machinery
> wandering through skyscrapers,
> Platinum-precious huntress
> insatiable.

The poem is matter-of-fact and disillusioned. But it is not heartless.

The miscellaneous poems which fill the remainder of the volume were reprinted in part from *Poetry* and *The Little Review.* Some bear their dates of composition and have such satiric opening lines as "Why not pull a tiger's tail," "The papers said, a lovely lady—interred" and such unsentimental titles as "Animal dynamo velocity" and "Cafe Girls." Many of these poems were re-collected ten years later, in *Not Alone Lost* (1937).

The same year that McAlmon published *The Portrait of a Generation* (1926), he completed another long poem, *North America, Continent of Conjecture*. The new poem of about 1200 lines was somewhat longer than the *Portrait*. Though it was finished by the time McAlmon sailed for America later in the fall, it was not published until after his return to Europe, in 1929. He then brought out a small edition, printing only three hundred ten copies. Scarcely more than a pamphlet, it ran to forty-three pages and was rather fancy. Hilaire Hiler decorated it with eight woodcuts and a decorative initial, and the printing was clear and attractive. Although McAlmon's other books had been printed by Darantière in Dijon, this one was given to the Etabl. Andre Brulliard of Saint-Dizier to produce. *North America* got no wider distribution than McAlmon's other work, though Moss and Kamin finally offered it for sale in New York in 1932. Like McAlmon's other work, a few copies can now be located at various scholarly libraries about the country.

Like his earlier long poem, *North America* attempts to define McAlmon's world. It sets out to answer the question, How is North America different from Europe? in order to show what Americans are like, why they are the way they are, what central aspirations unite them into a body, turning them from a mass into a community. In short, McAlmon attempts to write a little epic from which the narrative has been left out. This is what he attempted in *The Portrait*. Demi-epics like this were common in McAlmon's generation—perhaps they are common in all generations—the most famous of them being Hart Crane's *The Bridge*. Yvor Winter's classification of that difficult poem includes McAlmon's simpler one: "The book cannot be called an epic, in spite of its endeavor to create and embody a national myth, because it has no narrative framework and so lacks the formal unity of an epic. It is not didactic, because there is no logical exposition of ideas; neither Homer nor Dante will supply a standard of comparison. The structure we shall find is lyrical; but the poem is not a single lyric, it is rather a collection of lyrics on themes more or less related and loosely following out each other. The model, in so far as there is one, is obviously Whitman, whom the author proclaims in this book as his master."[23]

All that Winters says of Crane's poem can be said of McAlmon's, except that McAlmon never proclaims anybody his master, let alone

[23] *Poetry*, XXXVI (1930), p. 153.

Whitman. McAlmon is more the "youth, agile and attractive, passing by without taking his hat off to anybody."[24] When his poem was noted in *Poetry*, the anonymous reviewer (Harriet Monroe) compared it to *The Bridge*, to *North America*'s disadvantage. McAlmon's "historical fragments— even without the organization necessary to a complete work—betray indiscriminate selection, careless understanding, and a reach too wide and too eagerly attempted to insure mastery. Vigor is present in many separate statements and excellent realism in several episodes, and one finds considerable control of structural and metrical variety, but the poem does not disclose a vision capable of utilizing these factors effectively, or with any assurance of the unity those large dimensions require."[25] Louis Zukofsky also regarded *North America* as a kind of epic, but his conclusion differs from Harriet Monroe's. Zukofsky had a particular axe to grind: the importance of his own work and the "Objectivist" movement that he headed (under the aegis of Ezra Pound). Zupkofsky writes: ". . . examples of the complexity of the epic not limiting their content to the U.S.A. are few: Eliot's Waste Land, McAlmon's Portrait of a Generation and North America, L. Z.'s 'The' and unfinished 'A,' and the greatest poem of our time Pound's Cantos."[26]

North America, Continent of Conjecture is a discursive poem in which McAlmon discusses in disconnected sections American history, the American people, Puritan and Jesuit beginnings in America, even American words. These various sections are separated by some lyrics entitled "blues" bearing such titles as "Historic blues," "Bootleg town blues," "Machine Dance Blues," "Cult religion blues" and finally "Indian of the Disenchanted Desert blues." Neither the expository passages nor the lyrics are successful. Too frequently the poem seems little more than dressed up prose. The "Blues" are supposed to suggest indigenous rhythms like some of Vachel Lindsay's verse, but they are insufficiently syncopated. They rarely get off the ground and are altogether too labored. Here is a representative expository passage, celebrating (and defending) things American:

> Puritanism and catholic zealotry were not born in America,
> no more than was avarice.
>
> They were, as are many things American, imported ideas.

The poem begins:

---

[24] Emanuel Carnevali, in a review of *Explorations, Poetry*, XX (1922), p. 157.
[25] XXXVI (1930), p. 112.
[26] "Preface," *An 'Objectivists' Anthology* (Le Beausset, Var, France, & New York, 1932), pp. 23-24.

North America,
a continent but limitedly apprehended,
has a novel interest by being
neither this nor that which can be labelled
in the light of history:—
a dark, distorted, tricky mirror.
into which, perhaps,
are cast new germinations in the process.

The poem shows a greater critical than poetic intelligence, and many of the incidental remarks it contains are interesting. McAlmon identifies the Kentucky mountaineers and the Louisiana Cajuns as our "contemporary ancestors," and he observes in passing that the extremes in our climate not only encourage continual social change, but lead to skepticism. He notes that Americans fail to distinguish between abstract and concrete nouns; they too frequently assume that words like tolerance, idealism and strength refer to things, like oil and greenbacks. These observations are put down with a kind a slapdash. Even though *North America* was one of his favorite works, one suspects that in the years it lay unpublished in his trunk, McAlmon did not often read it, let alone revise it. In spite of the fact that it is somewhat ironic, it is not so witty as *The Portrait of a Generation* and is consequently less readable.

North America, Continent of Conjecture is identified as an "unfinished poem." McAlmon maintains that since the "continent" is still unfinished, a chance for greatness still remains. It has not yet exhausted its possibilities. Such a theme—the possibilities of America—when tempered by a candid account of natural limitations, is fit subject for a big poem. But as usual McAlmon's initial conception is worthier than his execution. His was not a failure of imagination or of intellect; his failure, here and generally, was a failure of the will. He did not imagine more generously than his talent could execute; too easily bored, he failed to develop the possibilities of his ideas. These shortcomings are particularly evident in *North America*.

Since there were no more Contact Editions after 1929, McAlmon was forced thereafter to depend on other publishers. In 1932 Caresse Crosby issued his *Indefinite Huntress and Other Stories* as number ten in her series, Modern Masterpieces in English. Also in the series were two volumes by Hemingway, *In Our Time* and *The Torrents of Spring;* a collection of stories by Kay Boyle; Faulkner's *Sanctuary; Lament for Living* by Dorothy Parker; and translations of Antoine de Saint-Exupery's *Night Flight* by Stuart Gilbert; of Alain-Fournier's *Big Meaulnes* by Françoise Delisle; of Charles-Louis Philippe's *Bubu of Montparnasse* by Lawrence Vail, with a preface by T. S. Eliot; and Kay Boyle's translation of Radiguet's *Devil in the Flesh* with an introduction by Aldous Huxley. Most of these books were reprints or translations of previous editions, and they were distributed by Hachette, the great French bookseller and publisher. One would expect them to have reached a wider audience than McAlmon's Contact Editions, but there is no evidence that they did. The series was not the success it deserved to be.[27]

The Indefinite Huntress and Other Stories, a handsome little paper-backed book, contained seven stories of varying length and of uniformly high quality. Like the other volumes, it is made up mostly of pieces reprinted from previous publications.[28] The title story had never appeared elsewhere, and only a few sections from "Mexican Interval" had been printed in Dr. Williams's revived *Contact* in 1932. The remaining stories and sketches were old. This volume and *Distinguished Air* without doubt contain the best fiction that McAlmon published. If these stories are not as finished nor as intellectual as Kay Boyle's and Katherine Anne Porter's, they have their own distinctive flavor. And they are not commercial and they are not contrived.

McAlmon returns to the country of his youth in the title story of this volume, but his attitude toward the Great Plains differs fundamentally now from what it was in his earlier fiction. Here he is not primarily interested in the country; here the fictional personages are more important to him than the world that they live in. One comes away from *Village* and the other volumes of stories remembering the heat and cold of the plains, the provincialism, the monotony, the narrow morality. In the earlier books the country takes one's first attention because clearly the raw country shapes the people who occupy it. This is not true of "The Indefinite Huntress." Now the huntress, Lily, dominates the world she lives in. Although her character is in part determined by her provincial milieu, we are now more concerned with the results than with the provincialism itself. Our attention is directed to the single person, not to the shaping society. As time has passed, McAlmon's rebellion against the country of his birth has become a thing more of the head than of the spleen. McAlmon has turned from an indictment of a society to an examination of a character.

As McAlmon's indignation has cooled, so has his writing. He has become less involved in his fiction. "The Indefinite Huntress" may

[27] Bell, *The Black Sun Press,* pp. 11-12.
[28] (Paris, 1932).

have grown out of his personal experience, but the story is objectified and does not read like a page from his diary. It is a reasonable artifact embodying a unified attitude toward the world and it is carefully plotted. The story is divided into four sections of unequal length, and within each major division the action rises to a climax; each of these is subordinated to a general climax. One could wish that a single focus were maintained in all four, that one attitude toward a central situation were consistently stated, but in spite of occasional unevenness in emphasis, the story is neatly put together.

In the first section, Lily, a rawboned and potentially beautiful Swedish girl, by associating with city-bred Helga recognizes that her life lacks beauty and that she herself lacks refinement of sensibilities. Her inertia starts to give way to resentment. In the second section, the gentleness of Dionysio Granger, a twelve-year-old boy some four years younger than herself, calls up an answering gentleness in her. "It hurt to think he wouldn't understand how sweetly she felt about him, with agony in the feeling" (p. 14), we are told. In the third section of the story Red Neill, a rather tough man of the town, perceives the mild qualities in Dionysio Granger that Lily has responded to, and, because of the boy, becomes aware of Lily. Rather astonishingly, they marry, both hoping to find in the other some of the gentleness that Dion has inspired. They are disappointed and receive only limited satisfactions from their relationship.

The two of them make the most of their companionable, rather sexless marriage. Lily turns her attention more and more to Red's business—stock breeding—while Red withdraws from it, growing more and more indolent. Lily's horses require all her energies, and she and Red become increasingly prosperous. Suddenly Red dies, of pneumonia; and Lily, more alone and unfulfilled than ever, turns to Helga, now separated from her faithless husband. She hopes that someplace, with Helga perhaps, she can find some completion, some rest.

This is, as I say, one of McAlmon's best stories. Each of these characters has a distinct individuality which is sharply edged and freshly perceived. As usual McAlmon has imagined all these people for himself, not allowing himself to be influenced by stock responses. The background—the rural area and small towns—is faithfully drawn, and neither the place nor the people is oversimplified. Indeed these persons seem motivated by emotions and powers that we—and they— do not understand. In this respect the story is reminiscent of D. H. Lawrence: Red and Lily both yearn, as Lawrence's characters yearn, after some unidentified accomplishment. In Lawrence this is always connected with love, with sex. The yearning in McAlmon's story is associated with love, too. The ordinary human relationships available to Lily and Red, like the conventional human relationships in Lawrence's books, leave them unsatisfied. And like Lawrence's people, they do not know what to do about their discontent; they only recognize their unhappiness.

Late in the action of this story we are told of a dream of Lily's: "That night she dreamed of Dion, but in the dream he changed to Red, to Helga, to a horse, which became again Red, and she and Red were running up the sky. With a snap she felt herself falling into eternity, and awoke, startled, with a stale terror and sense of misery." In this dream all the various elements of the story are drawn together. McAlmon is saying, as usual, that a full life must shut out no major quality of human nature. Lily and Red are left unsatisfied because each supplies the other only a part of what he needs. Ideally Lily would find in Red what in her dream appears divided among Dion, Red, Helga and the horse; but she and Red can not seem to give each other the tenderness, the affection, the passion and the beauty that they yearn for. Though they try to supply each other's needs, the puritanical habit of the provincial world will not allow them to fulfill themselves. When the story ends, Lily leaves her farms and her village. We are not confident that in Europe, her destination, she will find that fullness which she could not locate at home.

The story has other dimensions. Readers interested in myth can see here the retelling of an ancient tale. Dionysio is such an odd name for a boy in the Middle West that it suggests that its bearer has a particular and special significance. The name is of course a variant of Dionysus, the god of revel and drama. One of the well-known stories about him deals with Orion, the hunter; it and "The Indefinite Huntress" have notable similarities.

In the Greek story, Orion, deprived of his sight because of unfortunate love adventures, is aided by Dionysus and is taken by him to live with Artemis, the maiden huntress. After a time Orion dies, some say by Artemis's will. McAlmon's story recalls this myth. When we first meet Lily she is represented as coming from the fields; she is resolutely independent of men. We are reminded of Artemis. Red recalls Orion. He like Orion is a hunter, and in one episode takes Dionysio into the fields with him, an experience that the boy does not enjoy. After misadventures with "other Janes," through Dionysio Red comes to Lily as Orion comes to Artemis. Though Lily and Red marry, Lily like Artemis is never really "conquered by love"; Red, like the god, finds protection under the aegis of a virgin huntress. In time both Orion and Red waste away under their mistresses' superior, and essentially virgin, energy.

The parallels are insistent. It is as though McAlmon had received inspiration from the Greek myth and had domesticated it, moving it far from the Aegean to Twentieth Century Dakota. This mythic background gives the story an extra dimension, for it suggests that these American events have a peculiar inevitability. Because this action, now reported from America, has an analogous action in ancient times, we see that life repeats itself, and "The Indefinite Huntress" gains an unexpected grandeur.

Given its author's unclassical temperament, however, one suspects this whole Greek background is "added" as a kind of leg-pulling. It is doubtful that McAlmon wanted us to take it seriously. In his autobiography (written just following the publication of this volume, in 1933-1934) he speaks disparagingly of things classical. He wrote, "It is not unreasonable to ask if the Greek and classical tradition is not needlessly restrictive, because much fine literature has been entirely outside that tradition, as we are now discovering. . . . It is not suitable to a polyglot America, any more than it is or ever was to Russia."[29] McAlmon may have started a satiric story, intending to dupe the admirers of things Greek, and, in the course of the writing, got caught by his own fired imagination. As a result the leg-pulling joke turned into some of his best fiction. The story succeeds, of course, not because of its classical reference: it succeeds because it pictures a real world and real people moving and acting in it. But the parallels give it another dimension, a strength in depth.

The story is not different in theme from much of McAlmon's other fiction. As usual McAlmon insists on the primacy of the tender affections. As always, he suggests that the conventional world represses more than it liberates, and that provincial America represses most obviously. The classical symbolism of the story, though insistent, is in this view only a fillip. It gives the "intellectual"—McAlmon has no use for caviling "intellectuals"—something to talk about while worthier men participate in whatever life the story contains. McAlmon's little joke backfired, and most readers of "The Indefinite Huntress" will be glad.

---

[29] *Being Geniuses Together*, pp. 178-179. The whole passage is relevant: "That 'I am a poet, a bard, a singer' attitude has disposed many people to view poets as flighty creatures incapable of observing reality or of coping with experience, and it certainly has bred a spirit in the universities, which makes very precious lads and lassies indeed out of young people, who, if they must be poets, would be better poets using the idioms and symbols of their own time. We simply do not live on an island in the Mediterranean, where the sun flashes on the seas' wine-dark waves, like the reflection of lights on shining helmets. Greek gods and mythological figures mean nothing more than Hans Christian Andersen or Grimm characters to most." (pp. 179-180).

The second story in this volume is just as fine as the first. It is called "Green Grow the Grasses" and takes us again to the Dakota prairies. Unlike many earlier stories of his childhood, this time the first person narrator is not felt to be McAlmon. He is a created person, a character imagined by the writer. This story, no less than "The Indefinite Huntress," is objectified.

"Green Grow the Grasses" is the story of young, Latinate Antoine and his sweetheart, Enid. The two live instinctively, their uncalculated lives uncontaminated by the meddling intellect. We do not care that they are not married, for they represent a kind of spontaneity that the narrator cannot see in Rhoda, his overintellectual sister. The boy loses track of them as he grows up and only finds Antoine again in his late adolescence. By now Antoine and Enid have become, as it were, victims of a scheming world. Overworked and underpaid because Antoine has served a term in jail (rather melodramatically he had stolen money to pay hospital bills), they are worn and tired. Only a hint of the old insouciance remains in them. Unable to help them or their two children, the narrator moves on. Later he discovers that Enid has died in childbirth, with her third baby.

All this the speaker recalls when he sees an antique torso at Eleusis, that home of Attic mysteries, years afterward, and "suddenly Antoine was clear in my memory, as I had first adored him, as I last saw him, and then as he became." The carefree exiled Latin boy "had been to my awakening adolescence a symbol of faun-spontaneity with the clear sweetness of human relationships." For a moment the narrator is filled with indignation: "A wish to encourage him and what he stood for leaped within, and I wanted to know what had become of him. My rebellion asked why are such not given just enough calculation to be careful." But the speaker is no sentimentalist. To cultivate this indignation would do neither Antoine nor the speaker any good. "One can't let one's arrested-development emotions dominate however, so I forgot Antoine " (p. 73).

The point of the story is made both in the narrative and by direct statement. The good life, McAlmon thinks, must not discriminate against the passions. The intellect must not be set against the emotions; the intellect, by peeping and botanizing, should not destroy life in analyzing it. A full life includes both sensuous and intellectual pleasure, each in its place, each tempered by the other. McAlmon rejects the Puritan respectability of his Middle Western youth because its calculations destroy instinctive satisfactions. The organization of this story is admirable. Without awkwardness and without seeming hurry it unites action taking place over an expanse of time and space. McAlmon uses the technique of the first person narrative to real advantage; remembering, the speaker is able to unite events which occur at varied intervals. The prose style, like that throughout this volume, is "spontaneous" and particularly suited to its subject.

In the third story in this volume, "Mexican Interval," McAlmon considers a world which seems to set physical satisfactions above calculated restraints, but he finds that this too is dissatisfying. "Mexican Interval" is fictionalized autobiography. The protagonist, Kit, goes to a distant village in Western Mexico, and we observe his peregrinations through even remoter country areas. In the first section of the story Kit attends an Indian wedding where the groom, fired by strong drink, rapes his bride on the dance floor. In the next sections of the story he visits the local aristocrats who have an attractive pride of place. "I felt myself in a place where time didn't matter, and relativity had so arranged affairs that I was getting some quality of an armchair town's communal life, with the contemporary world and all its neurotic, nerve-driving, civilization of go-getters, easily accessible." These people, Kit thinks, have a quality which he lacks, for they accept life as he can not. "They don't soulprobe," Kit writes a friend. And yet when he observes the Goyceola clan gathered at a funeral, he knows that he has been romanticizing his experience: "This gathering is not Mexican; it is timeless, raceless," he says. "Romantic history and literature has been causing me to see this town and its people in the light of ancient Sumerian, Italian, Greek, or Egyptian towns, but coldly the business men descendants of old Goyceola reveal themselves as Babbitts, but harder Babbitts than the American type. They are distinctly suspicious of and on guard towards each other. Suddenly I realize that my stay here has been a vacation of variation only; it has not been release, and I don't want to escape from the world I knew before" (p. 144). By going into Mexico, Kit attempted to get into the prehistoric past, beyond the limitations of an overintellectualized civilization. But he could only discover that this world was not really different from the world that he had left.

If the Puritan world denied the dignity of spontaneity, McAlmon learned at last that the primitive world had its repressions too. There is in "Mexican Interval" and the stories of this volume a wisdom of resignation. If rebellion and indignation are emotions proper to youth, stoic acceptance is proper to maturity. In these stories McAlmon has grown older. Always capable of sympathy and objectivity, now his understanding deepens into compassion, and his rebellion softens into the beginning of acceptance. The rebellion, the indignation, flares now only momentarily, and then it sinks back. It gives color to all, but it scorches nothing. His spirit is not broken, but it is bent.

In 1933 and the first months of 1934, McAlmon was occupied with his memoirs, *Being Geniuses Together*. This long volume was not published until 1938, in London, and was McAlmon's last big writing project. The book begins with McAlmon's arrival in London, in 1921, and ends with his European wanderings ten years later. A gold mine of information about life in Paris during the Twenties, it has regrettably never been published in this country, and it has long been out of print. I have had occasion to pillage it more than once in the course of this essay. Although attractively gossipy, it created no stir when it appeared in England, perhaps because the British were more intent on steeling themselves in 1938 for the ordeal to come than for relaxing into a memory of the past. It contains character sketches of such people as T. S. Eliot, Wyndham Lewis, Harriet Weaver, J. W. N. Sullivan, Djuna Barnes, James Joyce, Ernest Hemingway, Ezra Pound, Ford Madox Ford, William Carlos Williams, Marsden Hartley, Gertrude Stein and many others, but McAlmon himself dominates the cast. If it is the function of autobiography to reveal the author, his habits, prejudices, foibles and strengths, this book admirably succeeds. If the book is overlong, and if the style is somewhat eccentric, these limitations are overcome by its vigor of writing, its freshness of observation, its independence of judgment and its constant wit. But most important, in the book McAlmon is drawn full scale, complete with all his contradictions and his charm.

McAlmon's only book to be published in the United States was a volume of poems, *Not Alone Lost* (New Directions, 1937). Of the thirty-two poems which it contains, more than half had appeared before. The collection was reviewed, with other "recent verse," by F. O. Matthiessen in *The Southern Review*. He wrote, "[McAlmon's lines about bullfights] demand comparison with Hemingway's *Death in the Afternoon;* and any juxtaposition would demonstrate the prose much more resiliently acute in its perceptions, its language far richer in its ability to evoke movement. These are just the superiorities of concentration which poetry must possess, and their absence reveals McAlmon as writing a bastard form."[30]

McAlmon might answer that he does not seek "concentration." He seeks to capture in words the impression of a single moment, a unique

---

[30] "A Review of Recent Poetry," *The Southern Review*, III (1937-8), pp. 368-369. Ten of the first sixteen poems, subtitled "Childhood," had appeared in *The Portrait of a Generation* (1926); four of the poems in the second section, "Jewels, Vegetables and Flesh," were reprinted from that same volume (two of them revised); the poems in "Tales of the Open Plains," the next section, had all appeared in various periodicals; and the last two poems, in a section called "Spain," had apparently not been published before.

experience. He attempts to put down a particular reaction to a particular circumstance:

> The blue heron flies north
> in the frozen sky, which floats
> an ether iceberg
> on the cold white plains. ("Away")

Sometimes the lines are discursive:

> Say then that life is grim
> beauty a fallacy, and an evasion
> amidst the debris of dying desire.
> Wonder too if love can be
> more than consummate futility
> through the blasphemy of time
> ("Say Then That Life Is Grim")

McAlmon's best poems combine the cause with the response, letting the image carry its own meaning. Poems like "The Crow Becomes Discursive" and "The Wild Boar" are the most successful of the collection. But Matthiessen is right. The poems in this volume fall short of the tightness that we ordinarily expect to find in good verse. The rhythms are loose, rarely achieving a sense of the inevitable, and the general terms—beauty, desire, futility—piled too close against one another, lead to an abstraction of thought which is reflected in a flaccidness of rhythms. A formal verse pattern would have sharpened and disciplined the lines.

The poems show an impatience with discipline. They celebrate rebelling bulls and boars and, sometimes, rebelling workers who react against "financiers." They are full of that old Romantic praise of revolution which leads to sympathy with the primitive, the untamed, the unorganized, with wild and dangerous animals. Though some of the poems contain now and again bits of irony and satire, more of them are without humor. McAlmon's earlier long poem, "The Revolving Mirror," is more satisfying than the poems of this volume because it is often funny. *Not Alone Lost* is a serious collection; it would be more pleasing if it were gayer. The last of McAlmon's volumes, it was nearly the last of his publications.

Miscellaneous Pieces

Though McAlmon published no books after 1937, scattered among the magazines of the early Thirties there is enough fiction to fill a good-sized volume. Some of it is as good as anything he ever printed.

McAlmon seems to have been cavalier about his own work. He apparently made little effort to get his volumes into the United States, where he might reasonably have expected to find an audience, and on several occasions he even let editors make their own choices from among his manuscripts. In 1932, when Peter Neagoe invited him to contribute to *Americans Abroad,* he let him take a section from an unfortunate amateurish novel which he had written long before.[31] He had printed a section from it in his own *Contact Collection* (1925). These are probably the worst pieces he ever published.

The periodicals received his best work. Three stories dealing with his memories of childhood are especially rewarding. "Potato Picking" and "The Jack Rabbit Drive" appeared together in Jolas's *transition* (1929).[32] Edward J. O'Brien put both on his "Roll of Honor for 1928 and 1929" and gave them both three stars in his Index. He reprinted "Potato Picking" in *The Best Short Stories of 1929.*[33]

"Potato Picking," a kind of plotless reminiscence, tells how Horace, age twelve, prepares to go to work harvesting potatoes, what experiences he has away from home, and what he finds when he returns. It is told from the child's point of view. Unlike many of the stories of childhood that are contained in McAlmon's volumes, in this story the boy has no opinions or perceptions that any bright youth might not have. Since the incidents are recounted as the naive boy sees them, and since he cannot yet understand the profound changes that adolescence is about to bring him—indeed is already bringing to one of his companions—the episodes have certain dramatic irony. The boy does not understand and scarcely notices the undercurrents which have significance for the reader. In the first episode, for example, a gypsy woman complains that her husband beats her; and, in the last, she has willingly returned to him. McAlmon· understands the psychology of this boy, poised in the last moment of childhood.

[31] (The Hague, 1932). The volume in which it appeared was something of a disappointment generally. Though it contained some of the important writers of the time, few of them gave Neagoe a selection of firstquality material. It contains, besides McAlmon, Conrad Aiken, Djuna Barnes, Kay Boyle, Whit Burnett, Malcolm Cowley, E. E. Cummings, John Dos Passos, James T. Farrell, Hemingway, Henry Miller, Pound, Laura Riding, Gertrude Stein, Williams and others. Although O'Brien placed it on his list of volumes of the best short stories of 1932, Samuel Putnam remembers fifteen years later that "when the volume reached America, George Jean Nathan promptly conferred upon it the distinction of being 'the worst book of the year.' A biased judgment, it may be, but—well, time has a way of deciding. Americans of the early depression were not impressed." (Samuel Putnam, *Paris Was Our Mistress,* New York, 1947; p. 237).

[32] No. 15 (Febr., 1929), pp. 84-93; pp. 93-101. The account of Jolas's delight in them is given in *Being Geniuses Together,* p. 248.

[33] (New York, 1929), pp. 159-168.

The companion, "The Jack Rabbit Drive," is even better. Horace, in this story age seven, and Sally, his playmate, gather beer bottles to sell so that they may buy candy. They gorge on money a bartender gives them to get them out of his saloon. Then, by accident, they observe the conclusion of a community rabbit-killing. Since the animals have become pests to the farmers, men, women and some children have banded together to drive them from the area. Horace and Sally see the slaughter of the helpless, jumping beasts; they see the dogs tear them to pieces and the farmers beat them into shapeless masses. Sally starts to take one of the dead animals home for her mother to cook.

"You aren't going to take that rabbit home, are you? You couldn't eat it, could you?" Horace says, and the girl replies:

"Why not? Mama feeds us rabbits lots of time."

"But it's dead," Horace explained.

"Every meat you eat is. That's what happens to all the cows that get shipped out of the stock yard every week."

Horace's mind was stalled . . . (p. 99).

That night Horace is pale, his mother notices, and he has nightmares.

"Potato Picking" describes innocence in a world where innocence can not last. "The Jack Rabbit Drive" is concerned with guilt. The two children both play where they should not, enter a saloon and take money from the saloon-keeper as they know they should not; observe the forbidden rabbit drive. Even when they—and the other characters in the story—do not act, they are inadvertently involved in some kind of group guilt. Thus the saloon-keeper by the children's presence in the barroom has a part, we are told, in their "guilt." And though the children see the rabbit hunt by accident, Horace feels "guilty" as a result. The people who are engaged in the drive are, like the children, caught up in a guilt they can not avoid. The rabbits in the interests of good crops must be killed; and yet the brutal killing of the harmless creatures strikes us all as horrible. "It isn't its fault it's nasty," Horace says, but the rabbit is killed nevertheless.

Both of these stories deal with the psychology of children, and as such they are valuable. But they are more. Basically they are studies of the inevitable and unavoidable guilt and innocence in which we are all involved. The innocence described in "Potato Picking" is sure to be lost; the guilt described in "The Jack Rabbit Drive" is inescapable. Beside the subtley of these stories, such stories as "The Lottery" and "The Portable Phonograph," also studies of guilt and innocence, look melodramatic and superficial. Their writing may be smoother, but already their professionalism begins to be dated. McAlmon's stories, whatever their faults, remain fresh.

The third of the uncollected stories of childhood is "Wisdom Garnered by Day" which appeared in *Life and Letters,* the distinguished British publication, in 1934. It is a reworking of material used ten years before, in a story that appeared in *This Quarter* in 1925.[34] It is the story of Benny's experiences at a colored revival meeting. The boy, his mother and brothers visit in Canada, near where, by some chance, there is a colored community. During the day Benny plays with Abie (Abraham) and Naps (Napoleon), sons of a shiftless and cheerful colored woman. The three boys run about the farm, observing a sow with her piglets, stealing honey from wild bees, talking of the cattle and the long Canadian winters. After supper, Benny escapes from his bed and goes with his older brothers to the colored revival meeting. His timidity overcome by curiosity, Benny creeps into the auditorium where a colored minister harangues his listeners about "de sin ob carnality" and "de blighting searing ruination which come from de obsession which is dat ob most ob my congregation." The congregation becomes increasingly hysterical until Eliza, a gentle washerwoman, becomes irrational. With eyes rolling and blood dripping from the lips that she had bitten, she rises and, stumbling down the sawdust trail, throws herself face down before the minister. Benny, frightened almost out of his wits, runs from the auditorium. "There were many questions he wanted answered, but he could not understand enough to ask them and knew surely that could he question he would not be answered. He didn't believe that older people could answer the questions in him themselves" (p. 165).

This version of Benny's experience is nearly twice as long as the earlier version. It contains nearly twice as many details of Benny's day about the farm; the account of the revivial meeting remains substantially unchanged. Though the story deals with powerful and perplexing youthful experience, it is not a story of "initiation," like Warren's "Blackberry Winter," Faulkner's "That Evening Sun," Hemingway's "My Old Man" and Anderson's "I Want to Know Why." In this story there is no dramatic realization of human complexity. Such a realization will come to Benny gradually, in good time. This story, for all its questioning, is only an episode in his continuous development. "Wisdom Garnered by Day" has an admirable tranquility. It ends: "The next day he could not quickly enough get to the Greens to tell Abie and Naps that he had been to the evangelical meeting, but his report of the experience was a sceptical one, endeavouring to convince the coloured boys that he was not taken in by that sort of

---

[34] *Life and Letters,* XI (1934-35), pp. 157-165; "Extract from Work in Progress," *This Quarter,* I, i (1925), pp. 167-172.

thing, not he" (p. 165). Nothing apparently has changed. And yet we see the lightning flashes of maturity on the horizon and we hear the rumble of distant thunder. The storms rise, but they do not break. Eventually Benny will understand what he has seen, as we understand it. But not now. Now the behavior of the colored woman at the meeting is like the behavior of the bees and the fish and the cattle: they are alike fascinating and alike mysterious.

These three stories are poignant because their protagonists remain throughout uninitiated into adult awareness. The parade of natural experience passes them; and in their innocence, these children observe from the sidelines. They are puzzled. An adult and daylight understanding awaits them.

McAlmon's best stories of young manhood are also buried in obscure literary quarterlies. "Blithe Insecurities" tells how Grant, restive under normal restraints, wanders foot-loose about the upper Midwest. Although the story appears in two parts in *Pagany* (1930-1931),[35] it had already been published in a different form as "Summer" in *A Hasty Bunch* (1922?). In this new version, Grant, impatient with his job in a flour mill in Minneapolis, goes to Duluth to hunt for work on the docks there. After a few days, his money having run out, he sets out to walk home to Minneapolis. A good part of the story is taken up with an account of the walk, the people he meets, the food he begs, the places he sleeps. At last he returns to his mother's kitchen. All this had been dismissed in a few sentences in the earlier version.

Gathering a few dollars by pawning a watch and selling some books, Grant next goes to Merivale, a small town in South Dakota where he had lived as a child. There he finds his childhood friends grown up. He has nothing in common with most of them; but with one, Sylvester, he now hits it off. Grant participates in the life of the community, drinking rot-gut with his friends in a deserted stable, loafing at the pool hall, dancing at a barn dance. He finds that he is as impatient with the small town now as he had been as a child. After some months spent working in the harvest fields beyond Merivale, he returns to the town, grown and matured and experienced. But he can not stay. He is filled with adolescent energy and discontent. In the end he tells Syl, "I feel as if everything were going to begin new and strange in my life. I can't go back to things. Except for mother I wouldn't even go to Minneapolis to say good-bye to the family. It isn't any place I intend to go, it's just cutting loose. I have to do

[35] I, 4 (1930), pp. 32-52; II, 1 (1931), pp. 60-81.

it" (p. 80). And he sets out with youthful cockiness for the unknown, forsaking his past.

Although the original version of the story was one of the best in its volume, this fuller, later version is better still. If the three stories of childhood contain a sense of perilous innocence, "Blithe Insecurities" contains a sense of adolescent restlessness. Grant "can't go back to things," for he is curious about the world; and stability, formal education, permanence are not attractive. He has already learned that what is important for him is not what is important for others. "O stick to law, Syl. You'll get as much satisfaction out of living your way as I do mine; more probably; but I can't plan and be cautious." Grant is coming to the beginning of wisdom: each man must find his own way, each must be true to his own nature.

"Blithe Insecurities" is especially rich in characterizations. Even the minor figures, Herr Max, Dr. Friedman, Dinkie Fahnstock, Marie Stearns, are not sketchy. As always in McAlmon's fiction, they are treated with considerable sympathy: McAlmon suffers fools gladly, in his stories. The situations have the ring of truth in them, and none are hackneyed or clichéd. "Blithe Insecurities" contains considerable understanding of the nature of young men; it contains a convincing picture of one young man about to set out to meet his fortune, and it is good humored.

McAlmon continued to rewrite his material. "New York Sleep-walking (The final chapters of a U. S. continental novel)" which he published in *Pagany* in 1931-1932 is a rewriting of *Post-Adolescence*.[36] This time, however, the rewritten version is inferior to the original. Grant now finds himself in Greenwich Village. He looks up Ellen Mowbray and, at a party for artists and writers, meets Sheila. When he goes to Sheila's apartment, she plays the piano in half-darkness. The stage is set, and he remains for the night. This is the beginning of an extended liaison. Though this first half of "New York Sleep-walking" has its virtues—candor, some interesting characters and de-tail—its central situation is essentially trite. Though the party is described honestly and Ellen Mowbray is seen in all her pathetic am-bitions, Sheila is like a woman out of the movies: beautiful, gifted, experienced and available. The hero is handsome and modest. Holly-wood's idea of Greenwich Village has got between McAlmon and his memory of it.

In *Post-Adolescence*, the earlier novel containing much of the same material, life in Greenwich Village was pictured with its poverty and gaiety mixed up together. In that earlier book, the young man

[36] II, 4 (1931), pp. 22-37; III, i (1932), pp. 87-100.

with his post-adolescent energies, enthusiasms and aspirations was the center of interest. It was a young book about a young man. "New York Sleepwalking" is different. These characters are only pretending to be young. They are not innocent, and they begin to look like roués. In *Post-Adolescence*, the characters drink as an expression of their exuberance, of their joy in physical pleasures; in the later version, they drink to escape the world about them, out of desperation. The newer story of Greenwich Village is better written than the first, its diction is purer, its situations are more fully developed. But it is tired and ultimately artificial.

The second half of "New York Sleepwalking" is no better. Though it is well organized, showing in each episode how isolated the characters are from one another and how futile their hopes of constancy must be, the central situation might have been copied from Noel Coward. Sheila and Grant have continued their liaison, accepting one another's careless infidelities. The situation is not salvaged even by their sophisticated recognition that this relationship can only be temporary, at best. The affair, Grant says, is his first. His behavior, however, belies his words. McAlmon tells the story of a young man's early experiences, but he gives him the understanding of a man of the world. The resulting story is not happy. Even though "New York Sleepwalking" contains the McAlmon virtues of disinterestedness and detachment, it is too slick, too conventional, to be as interesting as some of his other fiction.

The other stories which McAlmon published in periodicals are extremely various in quality. McAlmon says that *transition* in 1927 "published a few things of mine, Eliot Paul selecting one 'extract' from an early novel to show what a lousy writer I was in relationship to the other masterpieces of that issue."[37] This piece, entitled simply "Extract from Work in Progress," though more amateurish than the longer version previously published as "A Vacation's Job" in *A Hasty Bunch,* is not markedly inferior to fiction which McAlmon had had published with his blessing. A better story, though by no means his best, is "Deracinated Encounters," which was published in *This Quarter* (1927).[38] This too is labelled "extract" but no more of it appeared in print. It is the story of an American expatriate traveling in the Middle East. Alaric "groped for a center to his thoughts, suspecting that he was quite unprepared to grapple with what Egypt might mean to him." What he saw "gave him no greater sense of ghastly futility of life, ultimately, than he had felt in London, and

---

[37] *Being Geniuses Together*, p. 248.
[38] I, 3 (1927), pp. 204-241.

in New York, amongst highly educated, but terribly wearied people."
For, deracinated by choice, Alaric has no purpose: he is adrift. After
an account of his visit to Greece and Turkey, the story ends: "He
judged that the Eastern sense of fatalism, if as strong as it is supposed
to be, is indeed necessary to go on bearing existence in much of the
East, Egypt, Turkish hinterland. Fatalism or an animalic semi-
barbarism of combative savagery may be the essential answer" (p. 242).

"Deracinated Encounters" is a picture of a rootless man who,
having rejected his heritage, finds nothing else to which he can be
loyal. He sees the world without a consistent point of view, and tries
on each regional and national prejudice as though it were a garment.
If the plotless story is too long, its characters are well drawn and its
sense of place is sharp. It is, of course, autobiographical.

There are a group of three stories which have Paris as their locale.
Though they are not so completely autobiographical as those I have
just been discussing, in all of them McAlmon appears as the observer-
narrator. "It's All Very Complicated," a wrily funny story, deals with
Jeff, a Lesbian, who, tiring of other women, seduces Sam.[39] Sam is a
newcomer to Paris from the American South. When she fails to find
her experience with him satisfying, Jeff discards him, and Sam is hurt
by her casual desertion. The speaker explains: "You don't realize the
virginal quality of male nature. What man wants to feel ruined and
wronged when he thinks it's his province to do the wronging?" (p. 79).
Though the story contains too much undigested exposition, it is funny.
"The Highly Prized Pajamas," another story of Paris, is also funny,
and it is better organized. Yoland, a hard, bright young prostitute, is
taken up by Stout. Stout, a Canadian, is "sentimental," and wants
to marry her, an idea which strikes her as ridiculous. He showers her
with gifts, promising to send her money from America. But when
she asks for his pajamas, he will not give them to her. Since she had
worn them during their times together, he prizes them. The various
characters in this story are well drawn, and the milieu in which all this
takes place is beautifully explicated. The incident on which this story
was based was well known at the time.

"In-Between Ladies," the third story of Paris, is quite different
in tone.[40] Whereas the others had a kind of *joie de vivre,* reflecting a
sophisticated pleasure in the observation of human nature, in this story
the old curiosity is replaced by a kind of desperation. The party is
over and the hangover remains. Sven, the narrator, is in Paris re-
covering from an illness. He observes Lydia and other ladies of some-

---

[39] *Contact,* I, 1 (1932), pp. 64-79.
[40] *The New Review,* I, 4 (1931-32), pp. 371-382.

what unsettled virtue searching for men who can give them new thrills. They are no longer lovely, and they find that they must often buy their pleasures. They pick up Howard, a young American who has come to Paris "to write." Howard has found that his money is going fast. "If the old man doesn't send me money I'm apt to be one of those gigolo boys, if I can stand the racket," he says. "Hell, I don't know what I want any more. I used to think I was a serious man with ambitions. . . ." Sven tells him, out of his considerable experience, "If you're wise, you'll miss the summer season here. Once you get started on night life it's hellish hard to stop" (p. 48). This story is acrid, for here are none of the old pleasures in the panorama of experience. The jazz era is over; the time, 1931.

One of McAlmon's finest stories, "A Romance at Sea," dramatizes the wisdom to be gained on the other side of the jazz age.[41] The narrator, McAlmon himself, finds only one companion on his English ship with whom he can strike up a friendship. She is an ancient maiden, Miss Forbes, who has lived such a sheltered life in her English village that she is unacquainted even with the phonograph. Instinctively she trusts the speaker, and he plays records for her pleasure. When he gets off the ship at Los Angeles, Miss Forbes remains, to go, unannounced, to visit a friend in Vancouver. The story ends: "I find Miss Forbes has left more impression on my mind than most people I have encountered aboard ship. And why? She was only naive and simple and old, and her life had been without events. Was it that which disturbed me: that with all the chasing and turmoil and struggle for excitment and adventure one's capacity for enjoyment grows no larger?" (p. 33). The explicit wisdom of this story had been implied even in the first of McAlmon's stories. "Your ways and my ways are not the same," McAlmon's alter ego, Grant, had said, "and mine is no better than yours." Could it be true that life is as pointless as that, that no values exist at all, even the values of personal satisfaction? Can our search only show, McAlmon asks, that there is nothing to search for? Would his life have been as free if he had stayed home, tending his own garden?

Not much of McAlmon's writing remains unaccounted for—none of it fiction—only a few pieces of criticism and a few poems. Aside from his essay on James Joyce, his two pieces dealing with Gertrude Stein are his most important critical essays.[42] On Ford's invitation,

---

[41] *Pagany*, I, iii (1930), pp. 28-33; retitled "Machine Age Romance" in *The Indefinite Huntress and Other Stories.*

[42] "New American Literature," (London) *Outlook*, 58 (Aug. 28, 1926), pp. 191-192; quoted in *Being Geniuses Together*, pp. 137-138; "Gertrude Stein," *The Exile*, 4 (1928), pp. 70-74; quoted in *Being Geniuses Together*, pp. 139-142.

McAlmon contributed to a "Conrad Supplement" to *the transatlantic review* shortly after Conrad died.[43] He also contributed an account of Bastille Day to Pound's *The Exile*.[44] In it one can see his old insouciance. McAlmon's only considerable uncollected poem appeared in *Pagany* (1930).[45] Called "New England Victorian Episodes," it is a character study of "Pennythinker." Pennythinker, a New England painter, sees the world in terms of forms and colors and Watteau. Pennythinker says:

> Life as an idea is all right. I want no reality.
> Give me the divine trivialities,
> The little, exquisite emotions over flowers, perfumes,
> sounds, movement, color—and youth.

The poem is a satire of the Henry James—T. S. Eliot—Marsden Hartley type of intellectual who anatomizes life until no life remains. Pennythinker prefers to observe life from the sidelines, refusing to participate in the world's game, yet claiming the world's affections. His work, McAlmon says, is overintellectualized, oversensitized, supercilious and "arty." There are clear references to Eliot in the poem, even echoes of celebrated lines, like:

> Eagle without a cliff, he descended from thwarted heights
> to smile on gorgeous youth . . .

and

> Wind, vulgarly blowsy, swirling
> blew elemental tang upon bourgeois streets
> in whirlpools of dust, papers, odors
> stenched with a kitchen nostalgia.

The rhythms are pretty prosy, but they are consistent and real, and they create the character of Pennythinker admirably. The poem shows McAlmon's habitual contempt for the writers who *look* at life rather than *live it*. If it is slapdash, it at least has some of the joy that Pennythinker lacks. But the competition for attention, let alone im-

---

[43] II, 3 (Conrad Supplement) (1924), pp. 343-344. Hemingway's contribution to the series caused a scandal. He was himself acting as editor during Ford's absence, Ford having befriended him, much as Sherwood Anderson had befriended him earlier. Hemingway concluded his "appreciation" of Conrad with praise of Conrad at Ford's expense: "And now he [Conrad] is dead and I wish to God they would have taken some great, acknowledged technician of a literary figure and left him to write his bad stories." Ford later remarked that he had never attempted to assist a young writer but that the young person had not turned at the first opportunity and kicked him in the face.

[44] "Truer than Most Accounts," *The Exile*, 2 (1927), pp. 40-86.

[45] I, i (1930), pp. 25-30.

mortality, being so keen, this jolly poem will surely remain in obscurity. It will delight those few readers who find it, buried as it is in its defunct quarterly.

McAlmon's published work is by no means all he wrote. In his autobiography he speaks of an unpublished novel, "Family Panorama," which has never appeared. There remains much unpublished manuscript among his papers. When he died he had elaborate plans for revising *Being Geniuses Together* and his fiction, but it seems unlikely that he could have realized them even if he had lived. The last twenty years of his life were not productive.

*   *   *

Because of his insistence on immediate reactions to experience, McAlmon never acquired what the Twentieth Century has come to regard as the basic tools of the craft of fiction. His diction is impure by most standards, fluctuating from the colloquial to the archaic in a single sentence. His narrative conversation strikes the ear accustomed to Hemingway as drawn out. Since he is reluctant to dramatize action *within* fiction more than he observes it dramatized *outside* fiction, frequently his scenes trail off, their points unmade. In short, McAlmon fails to recognize that the conventions of fiction are only conventions. He mistakes the conventions for the truth, and in rejecting them rejects the necessary disciplines of art. McAlmon saw, for example, that the love with which stories deal is not generally so demanding outside fiction as within it. He assumes therefore that the love story falsifies experience. Of course it does not. Commonly the love story is used to illustrate the author's view of his world and his characters. The fictional love affair is conventional in that it suggests more than it itself is. McAlmon failed to see that situations and details in stories often have a greater importance than their intrinsic worth. He sometimes could not see the woods for the trees.

And yet if McAlmon cannot take a place among the foremost novelists of his time—Hemingway, the early Dos Passos, Faulkner— his writing at least has a quality distinctly its own. One can easily spot it. McAlmon stubbornly refuses to pander to established tastes. He attempts to please no group or society. He tries to record only what he himself knew of the world. When he strove to be free of cultural restraints, he attempted to be free of all emotional and imaginative bias but what his own experience forced upon him. He thought that a life shaped by another's imagination was a life of illusion; and he wanted no illusions, certainly none born of books. He refused homage to many of the accepted writers, for the life they described seemed artificial to him when measured by his own experience. They seemed to him poseurs who had failed to break through conventional habits of mind in order to arrive at genuine observation. In rebelling against the established culture and aesthetic, he attempted to come to the very heart of genuine experience. McAlmon strove to be Adam.

As a result of his rebellion against accepted deceptions, McAlmon seemed hardboiled. He seemed tough, for he found sentiment more pretended than felt in his world. Like Hemingway, he had come to distrust the tall words; their meaning had gone out of them. Talk was empty, he thought, and life was to be lived, not examined. He was no cynic; he never denied the possible validity of the passions. He thought only that they were more important than descriptions of them. The life lived took precedence over the life constructed, even in a work of art; and a genuine work of art reflected a full-blooded, living man.

Taken all in all, McAlmon's books are valuable to the Twentieth Century. This fiction can be profitably read as a supplement to the work of other writers of this time. We are not likely to find a better picture of Bohemian life in Greenwich Village than his *Post-Adolescence,* nor a more authentic picture of Middle Western America than his stories and novels of Wentworth and Merivale. His fiction corrects the professional treatment of his period. Pound was fond of comparing him to Sinclair Lewis. McAlmon's books are less finished than Lewis's commercial satire. They are more honest, for they do not dodge social and psychological complications. They question the very bases on which the society exists. Lewis's books, at last, are a subtle sort of flattery; McAlmon's are not. McAlmon sees much more than Lewis, and he reports it.

If the writing is less commercial than Sinclair Lewis's, it is less polished than Glenway Wescott's. Wescott, like McAlmon, constantly harks back to the country of his youth, that country which the war and the machine destroyed. But in Wescott's books, a dreamy boy sits listening to his grandmother's tales; in McAlmon's, a young scamp snitches his neighbor's apples. McAlmon's books have more undisciplined life in them than Wescott's. His are a man's books and they are filled with a man's energy. At best McAlmon's books have a masculine vigor and they have dash. Who touches them touches a man: this is both their virtue and their fault. They are spontaneous and candid and independent, and they record the journey of a lost soul, wandering between two worlds. They record an experience not peculiar to McAlmon nor to his country: some men from every generation revolt against their fathers in search of new ways of feeling and acting. Some are always dissatisfied with their inheritance. McAlmon was one of these free souls. Men of fierce integrity being rare, he does not deserve oblivion.

[handwritten margin note: he is not a poser]

[handwritten margin note: he is also very much his father]

appendix

CONTACT EDITIONS including books printed at the THREE MOUNTAINS PRESS

Unless otherwise noted, all books in the following list were printed by Maurice Darantière at Dijon. William Bird turned out on a hand press all books labelled solely THREE MOUNTAINS PRESS unless otherwise noted. All books were produced in editions of about three hundred copies. They are arranged here in order of publication.

1922?

A Hasty Bunch by Robert McAlmon.
Not dated; no place or publisher given.

1923

A Companion Volume by Robert McAlmon.
Published by Contact Publishing Co.
Not dated; no place given.

Post-Adolescence by Robert McAlmon.
Published by Contact Publishing Co.
"Written previously to A Hasty Bunch in 1920"
Not dated; no place given.

Two Selves by Bryher.
Published by Contact Publishing Co., 1923.
No place given.
Distributed in New York by Chaucer Head Bookshop.

Lunar Baedecker by Mina Loy.
Published by Contact Publishing Co., 1923.
No place given.
Distributed in New York by Chaucer Head Bookshop.

Three Stories and Ten Poems by Ernest Hemingway.
Paris; published by Contact Publishing Co., 1923.
Hemingway's first volume.

Twenty-five Poems by Marsden Hartley.
Paris; published by Contact Publishing Co., 1923.
Distributed in New York by Chaucer Head Bookshop.

Spring and All by William Carlos Williams.
Paris; published by Contact Publishing Co., 1923.

(The following six books were published in this order as a series. Ezra Pound served as editor.)

Indiscretions or Une revue de deux mondes by Ezra Pound
Paris, Three Mountains Press, 1923.

Women & Men by Ford Madox Ford.
Paris, Three Mountains Press, 1923.
Bird hired this book printed outside his shop.
Distributed in New York by Chaucer Head Bookshop.

Elimus: a story by B. C. Windeler.
Twelve designs by D. Shakespear and frontispiece engraved by Robert Dill.
Paris, Three Mountains Press, 1923.
Distributed in New York by Chaucer Head Bookshop.

The Great American Novel by William Carlos Williams.
Paris, Three Mountains Press, 1923.

England, by B. M. G. Adams.
Paris, Three Mountains Press, 1923.

1924
in our time, by Ernest Hemingway.
Paris, Three Mountains Press, 1923.
Appeared March, 1924.
Published in a revised edition as *In Our Time,* in New York, by Boni & Liveright, 1925; in London, Jonathan Cape, 1925.

Antheil and the Treatise on Harmony by Ezra Pound.
Paris, Three Mountains Press, 1924.
Printed for the author by Maurice Darantière, Dijon.
Publisher's label affixed without Bird's permission.
Republished "with supplementary notes" in Chicago by P. Covici, Inc., 1927.

Village: as it happened through a fifteen year period by Robert McAlmon
Published by Contact Publishing Co., 1924.
No place given.

A Draft of XVI. Cantos of Ezra Pound for the beginning of a poem of some length, now first made into a book, with initials by Henry Strater.
Paris, Three Mountains Press, 1925.
Only ninety copies printed.
This was the first appearance of any part of this poem in book form.

1925

Contact Collection of Contemporary Writers
No place or publisher given, 1925.
"Dedicated to Miss Harriet Weaver."
Containing selections of "works in progress" by Djuna Barnes, Bryher, Mary Butts, Norman Douglas, Havelock Ellis, F. M. Ford, Wallace Gould, Ernest Hemingway, Marsden Hartley, H. D., John Herrman, James Joyce, Mina Loy, Robert McAlmon, Erzra Pound, Dorothy Richardson, May Sinclair, Edith Sitwell, Gertrude Stein, W. C. Williams.

Ashe of Rings by Mary Butts.
Paris, Contact Editions, Three Mountains Press, 1925.
Published in New York by A. & C. Boni, 1926; a revised edition was published in London by Wishart & Co., 1933.

My First Thirty Years by Gertrude Beasley.
Paris, Contact Editions, Three Mountains Press, 1925.

A Hurried Man by Emanuel Carnevali.
Foreword by Dorothy Dudley.
Paris, Contact Editions, Three Mountains Press, 1925.
Distributed in New York by Chaucer Head Bookshop.

The Making of Americans by Gertrude Stein.
Paris, Contact Editions, Three Mountains Press, 1925.
Published in New York by A. & C. Boni, 1926.

Distinguished Air (Grim Fairy Tales) by Robert McAlmon.
Paris, Contact Editions, Three Mountains Press, 1925.
Printed by Bird by hand.

1926

Palimpsest by H. D.
Paris, Contact Editions, 1926.
Published in New York by Houghton, Mifflin, & Co., 1926.

The Portrait of a Generation by Robert McAlmon.
Paris, Contact Editions, Three Mountains Press, 1926.
Only two hundred of these were printed.

The Eater of Darkness by Robert M. Coates.
Paris, Contact Editions, 1926.
Published in New York in a revised edition by The Macaulay Co., 1929.

The Herdboy by H. Krebs Friend.
Paris, Three Mountains Press, 1926.
Bird disclaims any knowledge of this book. Presumably Friend printed it before the press was taken over by Nancy Cunard. The publisher's label was used without Bird's permission.

1928

Ladies almanack, showing their signs and their tides; their moons and their changes; the seasons as it is with them; their eclipses and equinoxes; as well as a full record of diurnal and nocturnal distempers. Written & illustrated by a lady of fashion [Djuna Barnes].
Paris, printed for the author, 1928.
1000 copies printed.
McAlmon saw this book through the press, but it is not properly part of the production of Contact Publishing Co.

1929

North America, Continent of Conjecture by Robert McAlmon.
Decorations by Hilaire Hiler.
Paris, Contact Editions, 1929.
Printed by Etabl. Andre Brulliard, Saint-Dizier.
310 copies were printed.

Sailors Don't Care by Edwin M. Lanham.
Paris, Contact Editions, 1929.
510 copies were printed.
Subsequently published in New York in a revised edition by J. Cape & H. Smith, 1930; in London, Jonathan Cape, 1930.

Quaint Tales of the Samurai by Saikaku Ibara.
Translated by Sen Kato.
Paris, Contact Editions, 1929.

1931

The Dream Life of Balso Snell by Nathanael West.
Paris and New York, Contact Editions, 1931.
Printed in the United States of America.
500 copies were printed, 300 for sale in America and 200 for sale in Great Britain and on the continent. Contact Editions had passed into the hands of Moss & Kamin, booksellers, who brought out this single volume. McAlmon was in no way responsible for it.

THE PUBLISHED WORKS OF ROBERT McALMON

I. BOOKS

1921
Explorations
London, The Egoist Press.
Poems and prose meditations.

1922
A Hasty Bunch
[Paris; Contact Publishing Co.] Undated.
Stories and prose meditations.
Contains: Backslider; Sing the Baby to Sleep, Marietta; Light Woven into Wavespray; Obsequies for the Dead; Elsie; A Boy's Discovery; The Baby of the Family; Three Girls; Filling the Pulpit; The American Critic; From Maine; Temperament; The Town Builder; The Psychoanalyzed Girl; The Fast Girl; A Business Family; Abrupt Decision; A Vacation's Job; New-York Harbour; The Little Ninny; Summer; Snow; The Futility of Energy; Momentary Essays: Skyscrapers, Morality, Portraits of Religious Ones, Frosted Fruit, Flame of a 'Youth,' A Poetess, Salesmanship, The Penny; Creation.

1923
A Companion Volume
[Paris] Contact Publishing Co., Undated.
Stories.
Contains: Putting a Town on the Map; A North Dakota Surveying Party; What Is Left Undone; The Spectators; An Illiterate but Interesting Woman; Three Generations of the Same; Evening on the Riviera, the Playground of the World; The Moving Picture Crew; One More to Set Her Up; Aunt Mary; The Advertising Agency.

Post-Adolescence
[Paris] Contact Publishing Co., undated.
"Written previously to A Hasty Bunch in 1920."
A novel.

1924
Village: as it happened through a fifteen year period
[Paris] Contact Publishing Co.
A novel.

1925
Distinguished Air (Grim Fairy Tales)
Paris, Contact Editions at the Three Mountains Press.
Stories.
Contains: Distinguished Air; Miss Knight; The Lodging House.

1926
The Portrait of a Generation
Paris, Contact Editions, Three Mountains Press.
Poems.
Contains "The Revolving Mirror."

1929
North America, Continent of Conjecture
Paris, Contact Editions.
An "Unfinished Poem."

1932
The Indefinite Huntress and Other Stories
Paris, Crosby Continental Editions, The Black Sun Press.
Modern Masterpieces in English, 10.
Stories.
Contains: The Indefinite Huntress; Green Grow the Grasses; Mexican Interval; Machine-Age Romance (formerly "A Romance at Sea"); New-York Harbour; The Laughing Funeral (formerly "Obsequies for the Dead"); Temperament; Evening on the Riviera, Playground of the World.

1937
Not Alone Lost
Norfolk, New Directions.
Poems.

1938
Being Geniuses Together
London, Secker and Warburg.
An autobiography.

II. CONTRIBUTIONS TO PERIODICALS
1919

"Flying: Aero-Laughter, Aero-Metre, Consecration, Consummation, Volplanetor, Perspicuity," *Poetry*, XIII (March, 1919), 317-321. "Aero-Metre" and "Aero-Laughter" reprinted in *The Literary Digest*, 61 (April 5, 1919), 40; "Aero-Laughter" reprinted in *The Independent*, 98 (April 26, 1919), 125.

1920

"Essentials," *The Little Review*, VII, 3 (Sept.-Dec., 1920), 69-71.
"[Credo]," *Contact*, 1 (Dec., 1920), 1.
"The Via Dolorosa of Art: White Males, Today's Music, Form Destructionist-Sculptor," *Poetry*, XVII (Dec., 1920), 117-129.

1921

"Modern Artiques," *Contact,* 2 (Jan., 1921), 9-10.

"Superwoman," *Contact,* 2 (Jan., 1921), 8.

"The Blue Mandrill," *Contact,* 2 (Jan., 1921), 8.

"Contact and Genius," *Contact,* 4 (Summer, 1921), 16-17.

"White Males"; "The Wild Boar," *The Tyro,* I, 1 (1921), 6, 12 (back cover).

1922

"Blackbird," *The Bookman* [New York], 54 (Febr., 1922), 587.

1923

"What Is Left Undone," *The Little Review,* IX, 4 (Spring, 1923), 32-43

1924

"Elsie," *the transatlantic review,* I, 1 (Jan., 1924), 59-64.

"Three Generations: The Same," *The Little Review,* X, 1 (Spring, 1924), 43-57.

"Away," *The Bookman* [New York], 59 (July, 1924), 532.

"Joseph Conrad," *the transatlantic review,* II, 3 (Conrad Supplement), (Sept., 1924), 343-344.

"[Extract from] Village," *the transatlantic review,* II, 6 (Dec., 1924), 655-661.

"Three Poems: How variously in France . . .; Brothers; The black cat loops . . . ," *The Little Review,* X, 2 (Autumn-Winter, 1924, 1925), 3-9.

1925

"Extract from Spring Leaves Again to Consider," *Contact Collection of Contemporary Writers* [Paris: Contact Publishing Co.], 195-213.

"Extract from Work in Progress, [Benny at the Revival Meeting]," *This Quarter,* I, i (Spring, 1925), 167-172.

"Contributions: Completion, For Instance, Query," *Poetry,* XXVII (Oct., 1925), 12-15; "Completion," reprinted in *The Literary Digest,* 87 (Oct. 31, 1925), 32.

"The Bullfight," *The New Coterie,* 1 (Nov., 1925), 49-51.

"Extract from 'Transcontinental,' " *This Quarter,* I, 2 (Winter, 1925-1926), 124-155.

1926

"New American Literature," (London) *Outlook,* 58 (Aug. 28, 1926), 191-192.

1927

"Deracinated Encounters," *This Quarter*, I, 3 (Spring, 1927), 204-241.

"Extract from a Novel [Ni in the Desert]," *transition*, 5 (Aug., 1927), 66-73.

"Truer than Most Accounts," *The Exile*, 2 (Autumn, 1927), 40-86.

1928

"The Revolving Mirror," *larus*, I, 5, 6, 7 (Apr., May, June, 1928) [one number], 10-39.

"Why Do Americans Live in Europe? [a symposium]," *transition*, 14 (Fall, 1928), 98-100.

"Gertrude Stein," *The Exile*, 4 (Autumn, 1928), 70-74.

1929

"Tales from Childhood: Potato Picking, The Jack Rabbit Drive," *transition*, 15 (Febr., 1929), 84-101.

"Mr. Joyce Directs an Irish Prose Ballet," *transition*, 15 (Febr., 1929), 126-134; reprinted as "Mr. Joyce Directs an Irish Word Ballet" in *An Exagmination of James Joyce*, [by McAlmon and others], Paris: Shakespeare and Company; Norfolk, Conn.; New Directions; London: Faber & Faber, 105-116.

[Answer to Questionnaire], *The Little Review*, 12 (May, 1929), 52-53. (With photograph of McAlmon).

"Potato Picking," *The Best Short Stories of 1929*, Edward J. O'Brien, ed., New York: Dodd, Mead Co., 159-168.

"An Illiterate but Interesting Woman," *The New American Caravan, A Yearbook of American Literature*, Alfred Kreymborg, Lewis Mumford, Paul Rosenfeld, eds., New York: The Macaulay Company, 161-164.

1930

"New England Victorian Episodes: Pennythinker," *Pagany*, I, 1 (Winter, 1930), 25-30.

"The Crow Becomes Discursive," *The Hound and Horn*, III, 2 (Jan.-Mar., 1930), 212.

"A Romance at Sea," *Pagany*, I, 3 (Summer, 1930), 28-33.

"Blithe Insecurities," *Pagany*, I, 4 (Fall, 1930), 32-52.

"New York Harbour," *The Morada*, 5 [Dec., 1930], 8-12.

1931

"Blithe Insecurities," *Pagany*, II, 1 (Winter, 1931), 60-81.

"Fortuno Carraccioli," *Poetry*, XXXVII (Febr., 1931), 247-251.

"Green Grow the Grasses," *Front*, I, 2 (Febr., 1931), 97-107.

"In-Between Ladies," *Pagany*, II, 2 (Spring, 1931), 41-49.

"[Excerpts from] Fortuno Carraccioli," *The Literary Digest,* 109 (May 9, 1931), 24.

"New York Sleepwalking (The final chapters of a U. S. transcontinental novel)," *Pagany,* II, 4 (Fall, 1931), 22-37.

1932

"The Highly Prized Pajamas," *The New Review,* I, 4 (Winter, 1931-1932), 371-382.

"New York Sleepwalking," *Pagany,* III, 1 (Winter, 1932), 87-100.

"It's All Very Complicated," *Contact,* I, 1 (Febr., 1932), 64-79

"Mexican Interval (An Excerpt)," *Contact,* I, 2 (May, 1932), 40-51.

"Farewell to Alamos," *Contact,* I, 3 (Oct., 1932), 88-91.

"Leavetaking," Americans Abroad, *An Anthology,* Peter Neagoe, ed., The Hague: The Servire Press, 251-262. (With photograph of McAlmon).

"Child-Blithely," *An "Objectivists" Anthology,* Louis Zukofsky, ed., Le Beausset, Var, France & New York: TO, Publishers, 162.

"Historical Reminiscence," *An "Objectivists" Anthology,* Louis Zukofsky, ed., Le Beausset, Var, France & New York: TO, Publishers, 41-42.

1934

"Tales of the Open Plains: The Crow Becomes Discursive, The Race, The Blackbird, The Silver Bull, The City, Threshing Season, The White Wolf, The Mother, The Frost in the Corn, The Wild Boar," *The New English Weekly,* V, 10 (June 21, 1934), 228-230.

"The Mother," *The Literary Digest,* 118 (July 28, 1934), 28.

"Wisdom Garnered by Day," *Life and Letters,* XI, 59 (Nov., 1934), 157-165.

1935

"Gertrude Stein," *The New English Weekly,* VI, 21 (March 7, 1935), 431.

"[Excerpts from] North America: Continent of Conjecture," *The New English Weekly,* VII, 6 (May 23, 1935), 110; VII, 9 (June 13, 1935), 170; VIII, 1 (Oct. 17, 1935), 31.

Index